PATTERNS OF PETER AND PAUL

LISA JOHNSON

To Earl,

Thinking of you seems to turn up the volume.

What is it that makes us afraid of a mind
that shows us the way when our bodies are blind?
Control, control can we ever let go
of the horrible hold it keeps on our souls?

CONTENTS

Introduction

This is the third book that completes a trilogy of books I have written on God and our human consciousness. In the first two books, I establish that the Holy Trinity, as defined by Jesus and the Old Testament prophets, is the whole of the human mind. In this book, I seek to show how this central theme of the Bible was corrupted to make way for the creation of a new religion called Christianity.

It seems to me that Paul either purposely created confusion in his writings to make his fantastical message palatable to the masses, or he backed himself into a corner adopting a position that made no sense in the final analysis, and it forced him to make up the message on the fly. After filling my Bible with notes trying to make sense of Paul's disjointed thoughts and illogical conclusions, I decided to find an online Bible and copy all his letters into a text document that I could read through and make notes as I went along. Although it helped, it was still an effort fraught with frustration and confusion regarding interpretation.

The process of understanding Paul was similar to the process of understanding the true nature of good and evil that I underwent while writing *The Evolution of Good and Evil*. Nothing was clear until I began the process of approaching the Bible with a realistic view of human nature. Once I began interpreting the Bible in terms of our human mind which Genesis 1:26 says is made in the image of God, it was like untangling a huge ball of knotted twine. After concluding that the purpose of the Bible is not to describe a God without but instead to teach us how to find the God within, all the stories and characters came together in a cohesive narrative which describes the nature of our human consciousness and the relationship between our thinking and our behavior.

Paul's doctrine breaks with reality in the sense that it is premised on believing that a spirit was giving him his teachings and then having faith that Paul's word was good. It literally bypasses the faith in ourselves that the rest of Bible tells us to have and puts our faith in the lap of one man who claims over and over again that he is not lying. Paul conjured up the whole notion of a holy Spirit that is separate and apart from our own human spirit of life which Jesus made the core of his message when he referred to it as the kingdom of heaven within. (Luke 17:21) Paul broke the cohesiveness between the Old Testament and Jesus and not in the good way that is often labeled as the New Covenant. He destroyed eons of knowledge about the human mind and nature contained in the Bible which Jesus was clarifying for us so that we could apply it in a very tangible way to our own thinking and behavior. Jesus was creating a new paradigm for the future while Paul created a religion.

We do not need religious teachers directing us to an external god in three forms that has never existed. We need psychiatrists and psychologists to give us the framework that is sorely lacking in studying a book whose sole focus is the human mind. When Paul separated spirit from the human being and made it into something we can choose to accept or reject, he destroyed the cohesive message that runs throughout the Bible from Genesis to Revelation. His letters take a detour from the truth and to the extent that Christianity has adopted his doctrine, it too has taken a detour from the truth.

I have adopted a narrative approach to this book and have been purposely sparse in quoting direct scripture. I have, however, provided citations whenever referring to Paul's writings so that the reader can look them up him/herself to verify my interpretation of those verses. I tried very hard not to use the same approach Paul took in his letters of misquoting scripture and then spinning his misquotes to make them conform to his agenda of converting the entire Gentile world to his newly created religion which bore no resemblance to either Jesus' message or Jesus himself.

Of course, it goes without saying that my interpretation of Paul's writings conforms to a world view I have formed based on what I believe the Bible teaches us about our human nature of good and evil. Although I believe my world view conforms to the true teachings of the prophets and Jesus, it is up to the readers of this book to decide for themselves what world view they choose to hold. My goal in writing this book is not to destroy anyone's legacy. It is to restore truth and balance to a set of facts that were manipulatively created to further human agendas. If legacies are destroyed based on objective analysis, so be it. They were never meant to exist in the first place.

Prologue

Pilate was not a man to be toyed with. He was the one who played people. So, when Joseph of Arimathea and Nicodemus showed up in his chambers to tell him how the chief priests were paying off witnesses to remain silent about seeing Jesus alive, Pilate could not contain his anger at being made the fool. How could this man, Jesus, be alive? Why wasn't he told?[1] As he stormed out of his chambers, he ordered the two men to be held in custody until he could get to the bottom of it.

Pilot and his soldiers barreled into the synagogue ordering that all the temple rulers, scribes and doctors be brought before him. Caiaphas and Annas, the chief priests directly responsible for orchestrating the crucifixion of Jesus, knew they were about to come face-to-face with accountability. The intimidation, threats and blustering that worked so well in silencing their minions would serve to kill or imprison them with Pilate. The biggest mistake of their lives was about to blow up in their faces. They needed to come up with a convincing story line fast. If Pilate were to find out they intentionally orchestrated everything to put the ball in his court of executing an innocent man, their heads would be where they put Jesus'.

If they were to save themselves and retain their positions within the hierarchy of power, then claiming they were not aware of the facts until after the deed was done was their best defense. It was also plausible since only they and their trusted lawyer, Gamaliel, were aware of the truth. And so when Pilate ordered the doors shut and the books of the Temple brought before him, Caiaphas and Annas swore on their sacred book adorned with gold and precious stones that they did not know Jesus was the much awaited Messiah until after they crucified him. They told Pilate that it was only when it was reported to them that the tomb was empty and Jesus was seen walking around with his disciples that they opened their holy book and found an account that calculated the Messiah's coming.[2] With hands wringing, the two men swore on that very same holy book that when they discovered the timing of the Messiah in their holy book matched up with Jesus' arrival they were completely surprised. They would never have harmed a hair on his head if they knew it before sending him to Pilate to have him executed.

For a man like Pilate, that story was as plausible as the lies they originally came to him with about Jesus telling people not to pay their taxes. No ... these men had done the calculations long before the attempted killing because the calculations were the motive for sending Jesus to Pilate for purposes of executing him. But what could Pilate do about that now? If the truth came to light, he would look like an idiot who allowed himself to be used by a couple of Jews. The governor of the great Roman Empire could not let that happen. So, after writing down everything he was told and placing all the accounts in the public records of his hall, Pilate closed the book on the matter and ordered Caiaphas and Annas to shut up about everything and keep their Jews in line or suffer the consequences. Caiaphas and Annas breathed a huge sigh of relief and they, along with Gamaliel, came up with a strategy for silencing anyone who brought up the name of Jesus ever again. It was time to move on having achieved what they wanted to achieve. No sense risking any further inquiry into the matter by entertaining any discussion about it. Jesus was dead as far as they were concerned and that would be that going forward.[3]

[Note: In my book, 'The Mobbing of Jesus Christ, I make the case that Jesus never died on the cross. Many people in the post-crucifixion era, including the chief priests, the apostles, many Jews in the community and Pilate all knew this, and this knowledge drove their actions going forward]

1

The Creation of the False
Holy Spirit Doctrine

Live And Let Live

The short leash that Pilate wrapped around Caiaphas' neck made it very dangerous to even say Jesus' name in the post-crucifixion environment. Caiaphas knew that his power, and very life for that matter, was dependent on keeping Pilate happy. The best way he had for ensuring that Pilate's reputation was protected and his own position secured was to contain any talk about Jesus and what happened to him. The can of worms any discussion on the matter would open up could easily spark the flame of revolution if it became known he had tried to kill the Messiah. He also knew that the challenge of silencing all talk about Jesus was nothing compared to the tightrope he was walking trying to keep the truth from getting out that the Messiah was still alive and could return to Jerusalem at any time to complete his mission.

Caiaphas and the Sanhedrin operated out of Jerusalem. That is also where the apostles of Jesus were preaching. In Acts, Chapter Four, both the Apostles John and Peter are jailed and appear before the Sanhedrin for "teaching the people and preaching Jesus as an example of the coming back from the dead. " (Acts 4:1-3) Caiaphas decides to spare their lives for fear of a rebellion breaking out and releases the two men with orders "not to make statements or give teaching in the name of Jesus." (Acts 4:18) After going right back out and preaching again in the name of Jesus, Peter and John are hauled back to jail. When they appear before the Sanhedrin a second time, Caiaphas is furious that Peter and John have disobeyed his orders not to talk about Jesus and just as the Sanhedrin is about to have both men put to death this time around, their chief legal officer named Gamaliel advises them to tread lightly.

After clearing the room to confer with the chief priests in private behind closed doors, Gamaliel explains that Peter and John are not like the men who led previous movements which fizzled out after they were killed. These two men are direct followers of Jesus. If they are killed, the risk of rebellion is certain. He tells them the better course of action would be to let them live because Peter is preaching a message that bears no resemblance to that of Jesus, the Messiah. If the movement dies out on its own, so much the better. But even if the movement doesn't die out on its own, Gamaliel tells them, that too is okay because the message that Peter is giving is harmless.

> Acts 5: 38-40: "And now I say to you, Do nothing to these men, but let them be: for if this teaching or this work is of men, it will come to nothing: But if it is of God, you will not be able to overcome them, and you are in danger of fighting against God. And he seemed to them to be right: and they sent for the Apostles, and, after having them whipped and giving them orders to give no teaching in the name of Jesus, they let them go."

In Gamaliel's view, it was a matter of live and let live. He argued it was not worth making martyrs out of them and raising the ire of their followers when they were so much more useful to the power structure by remaining alive and keeping the focus on a dead Jesus instead of a very much alive Messiah. Peter was doing their work for them far better than they could ever do it for themselves. A dead Jesus who rises from the dead in spirit to save mankind is much better for the security of their positions than a living Jesus who could come back in town and reinvigorate a populace that thinks he is dead and gone – not to mention reinvigorate the ire of Pilate who was depending on them to keep the matter dead and buried.

The chief priests cannot argue with the logic. After calling the apostles back in, flogging them and again ordering them not to speak in the name of Jesus, the apostles are released thinking they have won a victory. Funny how it is that this court appearance is the last time that Peter or any of the apostles ever appear before the Sanhedrin even though Caiaphas was ready to execute them before Gamaliel stepped in and even though the very next verse says, "And every day, in the Temple and privately, they went on teaching and preaching Jesus as the Christ." (Acts 5:42) In fact, Acts 8:1 says that following Stephen's death, "A violent attack was started against the church in Jerusalem; and all but the Apostles went away into all parts of Judaea and Samaria."

It became safe to preach the holy Spirit doctrine that Peter and John were preaching. As we will see, Stephen preached the message that Jesus actually taught and it was directly responsible for his death, as opposed to the Apostles who were allowed to stay safe and sound in Jerusalem teaching about a man who came back from the dead. It was during this persecution, by the way, that the New Testament first introduces us to Saul, later known as Paul. He is the one entering house after house and imprisoning people in his attempt to destroy the church. (Acts 8:3)

If you are anything like me, you have probably never heard of Stephen before. He is not one of the more popular New Testament figures but just like Jesus, he was killed for what he was saying. In fact, Stephen's trial before the Sanhedrin reads like a repeat of what was done to Jesus. They brought in false witnesses to tell lies about what he was saying and when Stephen testified in his own defense, they became so infuriated at him that they didn't even wait for a conviction. They had him stoned as Saul/Paul looked on consenting to his execution. (Acts 8:1)

So what was it about Stephen's testimony that so infuriated the Pharisees? It could have had something to do with the striking parallels it had to the real message of Jesus "in the flesh." Whereas Peter was placing the emphasis of his message on a resurrected Jesus who sends the holy Spirit to those who believe in the resurrection, Stephen was giving the same message that made Jesus a marked man. He was making the distinction between the Moses who was sent to deliver the Israelites from slavery by giving them the Ten Commandments to guide them in their journey and the Moses who acquiesced to the Israelites' grumblings by appointing leaders over them who would tell them what to do with their laws. (Acts 7:34-42).

The distinction between Moses the deliverer of God's Ten Commandments and Moses the lawgiver of hundreds of rules becomes crucial in understanding the Bible in terms of what Jesus and the prophets were saying versus what the Pharisees and Sadducees on the Sanhedrin were pushing. In his trial before the Sanhedrin, Stephen tells the chief priests how Moses received the Ten Commandments from God who had witnessed the affliction of his people in Egypt and wanted to rescue them from it. (Acts 7:34) God did not send a man down Mt. Sinai to serve as the Israelites' ruler and deliverer. God sent them a set of rules that were delivered by a man.[1] Those ten commandments were meant to guide them into the promised land collectively when followed individually, but the Israelites rejected them in favor of a structure with which they were familiar. They pushed Moses aside and turned to Aaron to "make them gods who would be their leaders." (Acts 7:39. See also Exodus 32:21-23)

What I have found during the writing of this trilogy of books on consciousness is that this distinction is probably the most important distinction in the Bible in terms of a person's salvation and that is exactly what has made it the most dangerous in terms of a person's survival in organizations run by Pharisee-like god leaders who rely upon an Israelite-like slave mindset in their subordinates for their positions and power.

The chief priests of the Sanhedrin were the descendants of the human god leaders that the Israelites ask Aaron to appoint to rule

---

1   See Exodus 19:3-6: "And Moses went up to God, and the voice of the Lord came to him from the mountain, saying, Say to the family of Jacob, and give word to the children of Israel: You have seen what I did to the Egyptians, and how I took you, as on eagles' wings, guiding you to myself. If now you will truly give ear to my voice and keep my agreement, you will be my special property out of all the peoples: for all the earth is mine: And you will be a kingdom of priests to me, and a holy nation. These are the words which you are to say to the children of Israel."

over them. These man-appointed god leaders in the Sanhedrin were the ones who Stephen was addressing when he concluded his testimony by telling them that just like the god leaders before them who put to death the prophets who foretold the coming of the Messiah Jesus, they were now the betrayers and murderers of the Messiah himself. They received the Ten Commandments but they did not observe them. (Acts 7:53) One of those commandments was, "You shall not invoke the name of the Lord, your God, in vain." [Translate: You shall not appear to be righteous and good while you are acting with a mind that is corrupt and evil.] Another was, "Do not kill." And still another was, "You shall not bear false witness against your neighbor." [Translate: Lie] (Exodus 20:7, 13, 16) The human-appointed god leaders on the Sanhedrin broke all three commandments in their attempted murder of Jesus, all the while hiding behind their cloaks of righteousness as educated and holy temple leaders.

If there is anything self-righteous and evil hypocrites hate worse than having the mirror held up to their souls, it is having it held up by someone who has the moral authority to do so. In Acts 6:15, Stephen is described as having the face of an angel. Speaking the truth gave him the face of an angel. He not only talked the talk, he walked the walk and the chief priests in the Sanhedrin hated him for it because the truth was not on their side. The truth ruined the reputations they had so carefully crafted for themselves. The truth nailed them to their own crosses of hypocrisy, deception, murder, greed, vanity and lust for power. The members of the Sanhedrin became so incensed at Stephen's speech that they did not wait for a conviction. They had Stephen stoned on the spot for telling them something they did not want to hear.

The Jewish leadership couldn't handle the truth because they had become too attached to the power, money and influence the lie provided to them. Power is derived from control. They needed to change the focus from the God-given commandments of God to the man-made laws of Aaron and Moses because man-made laws feed the beast. They keep the hierarchy of power in place. Human god leaders who want to control rather than lead a community of people always need to change the focus from the commandments of God to man-made laws which dictate behavior because man-made laws give these god leaders their lever for exerting their power. Laws require a huge and complex network of enforcers, administrators and judges for their execution; all of whom report to the gatekeepers answerable to the leader(s) at the top of the power hierarchy. The more amoral and criminal the populations these enforcers, administrators and judges control, the bigger the bureaucracy becomes and the greater the power gained by these leader(s) of the pack who control the gatekeepers who control the enforcers, administrators and judges who control the population.

As I discuss in my book, *Morality Within the Framework of Reality*, Hitler specifically chose the hierarchical structure of leader/gatekeepers because it provides the optimal means of control over any organization of people.[4] No wonder the chief priests gnashed their teeth at Stephen and spit on Jesus. These two men had the capability of dissolving the illusion that killers, liars, manipulators, hypocrites, law breakers and thieves are better at controlling our conduct than we can ourselves if given the proper training and environments. The fact that many Jews were scattered to the regions of Phoenicia, Cyprus and Antioch after the killing of Stephen shows just how much the illusion was dissolving and reality was catching on.

The reason it was made against the law for anyone to claim to be God (say the kingdom of God is within) was because the chief priests and experts in the law knew it was the truth that Moses received on Mount Sinai, but which they had carefully manipulated out of existence by focusing on the man-made laws Moses was pressured to implement when the Israelites refused to police their own behavior. That is the only way any god leader can survive. They know their money and positions depend on people like the Israelites who have the hopeless and helpless mindset of slaves who depend on their masters to tell them what to do. We all instinctively know it's the truth, but our own slave mindsets have us believing there is nothing to be done about it.

Stephen was courageously teaching what got Jesus killed. He tells the Sanhedrin in Acts 7:53, "You received the law as transmitted by angels, but you did not observe it." The Ten Commandments are the law transmitted by angels, in Stephen's words, because they are the commandments of our human spirit that exists right there along with God and the angels. That's when the chief priests became furious and began grinding their teeth at him. Speaking truth to power is the most dangerous act a person can undertake in corrupt systems and societies because it puts the entire power structure at risk of being seen for the fraud upon the people it is. That's why just a few verses later, it says "they [the chief priests] cried out in a loud voice, covered their ears and rushed upon him together. They threw him out of the city and began to stone him. The witnesses to

Stephen's stoning laid down their cloaks at the feet of a young man named Saul." (Acts 7:58)

The chief priests had the same mindset as the Nazi judges who shouted down people of conscience in their courtrooms. The accused were not provided with an adequate defense and were vehemently called crackpots, traitors and mentally ill by the judges who had long since sold out their robes of justice to the Nazi ideology/theology of the state when they agreed to ask themselves at every decision: "How would the Fuehrer decide in my place?[5] Once they decided to follow the immoral and criminal dictates of the state in exchange for keeping their jobs, they gave up their souls. That is what our soul is. It is not some spirit guide. It is our mind's internal programming which gives us our natural sense of what is fair and just in our dealings with one another. We go against that programming at our own peril.

People like Jesus and Stephen are not willing to give up their natural programming that the prophets referred to as God. Their ability to make other people not want to give it up either is what made them so dangerous to the Pharisaic power structure that relied upon the replacement of that natural programming with behavioral and thought conditioning they administered and supplemented with the hundreds of Mosaic laws. As the god leaders who were in charge, they of course exempted themselves from the conditioning and laws they used to keep the Jewish population under their thumb of control. (See Matthew, Chapter 23)

Peter's Fetter of Forgetfulness

Unfortunately for him and humanity itself, Peter never got it like Stephen and Jesus did. The reason why Gamaliel told Caiaphas to let Peter continue preaching what he was preaching was because Peter's message was the childlike fantasy of a man who either never understood what Jesus was teaching him, or else he understood it all too well but was afraid to preach it in a truthful way for fear he would end up in the same place as his teacher and Stephen.

Peter loved Jesus the man. I have no doubt about that. I think it was his love for the man and his awful betrayal of that man that gave Peter his passion. However, I do not believe that Peter ever gained a passion for the message itself because Peter was a very egoistic man who was unable to change in the radical way required for dealing with truth. Surviving within hierarchical systems of authority and control more often than not requires us to remain blind to the truth if we want to survive. Adapting Jesus' message to his own mind would have required Peter to give up all the egoistic and chauvinistic beliefs he had acquired over a lifetime of living in a patriarchal society. It would have required him to see the God within himself so that he could see it in everyone else. That is a difficult process for anyone to undertake, but in a society like the one Peter was operating in - where an internal state of mind of arrogance, chauvinism, competitiveness, toughness, ego and machismo are valued assets in its male members – it is almost impossible if one wants to be able to care for oneself and one's family. The incentive to change those qualities for a more humble, cooperative, compassionate, conscious and egalitarian state of mind like that of Jesus just does not make sense for men like Peter when they do their personal cost-benefit analyses.

It is obvious to anyone who reads the Gospels of Jesus or the letters comprising 1st and 2nd Peter that Peter decided to nurture his ego consciousness over attaining a more Christlike consciousness. He never tries to hide his chauvinism in any of these writings, which leads me to believe he thought nothing wrong of it. (See 1 Peter 3:1-7 for his views on women) In Peter's mind, women were to be ruled by men. They were to be quiet and fade into the background where they may be seen but definitely not heard. The holy Spirit he claimed entered his heart upon his own declaration of belief apparently had little effect on his ability to view God as the equalizer of all human beings – male and female alike.

There is a striking passage in the Gospel of Mary where Mary Magdalene tells the disciples that Jesus told her, "In a world I was freed through another world, and in an image I was freed through a heavenly image. The fetter of forgetfulness is temporary. From now on I shall rest, through the course of the time of the age, in silence."[6] After she finishes, Peter accuses her of lying. He tells her and the other disciples that Jesus never would have told Mary something that he didn't tell the men. When Mary starts crying because Peter is accusing her of lying, Levi steps in and tells Peter he is always angry and his anger is making him treat Mary like an adversary. After telling Peter he has no right to question her if Jesus found her worthy, Levi tells the disciples they should put on perfect humanity as the Lord directed them and go out to preach the good news, "not making any rule or law other than what the savior indicated."[7]

The only two laws I am aware of that Jesus emphasized were the commandments to love God with all our heart, mind, strength and soul and to love others as we love ourselves. He said the whole law and the prophets depend on these two commandments. (Matthew

22:40) As you will see, Jesus' two commandments contrast sharply with the hundreds of laws the Sanhedrin imposed on the Jewish community and the dozens of rules that Paul eventually imposed upon the members of his churches.

Peter obviously left the room without a proper understanding of what the Lord's laws were. If he had understood them, he would have treated Mary with the respect she deserved and not as an object worthy of his scorn. It would have done Peter good to ask Mary what she thought Jesus meant by this saying instead of discounting her as a woman undeserving of having this information shared with her. A discussion about Jesus' saying may have helped him break through the armor of his ego that had him adapting to his external patriarchal environment instead of to his own consciousness within.

Mary was relaying to them Jesus' view on existence itself. When he says that in a world he was freed through another world, Jesus is telling Mary how he came to know the reality of God in this physical realm where we can get so caught up in the doings of our external environments that we can easily lose the connection with ourselves.

Our consciousness exists in time and space until it enters the physical realm where it must work through a physical brain. In *The Evolution of Good and Evil,* I discuss in detail how our brain creates a barrier in the sense that we come to view it and our five senses as our reality, rather than as a tool our consciousness uses to experience its physical existence. Instead of retaining a focus on our true existence as an eternal consciousness inhabiting a physical body for a certain length of time, along with the ramifications of that realization, we acquire a short-term focus on survival where our brains must learn to adapt to systems and environments we had no part in creating. It was Peter's brain that created emotions and thoughts to make him feel superior to Mary because that was what he was taught to feel and believe as a man in a patriarchal society where men are perceived as superior to women.

I think it was Jesus' belief that this process of a brain creating output for use in our physical world is what creates the false construct of reality. It causes us to forget our true existence as consciousness preexisting in time and space. Our time on this earth can translate into one huge waste of time if we fail to throw off the fetter of forgetfulness our external environments create with all their systems, beliefs, doctrines, ideologies and laws and refocus our consciousness on the long-term nature of our existence. If we are to be at peace with ourselves in this world, Jesus tells us we must free our consciousness from *the fetter of forgetfulness* which begins as soon as we exit the womb and begin learning how to conform to our respective environments however they may be set up. It is only when we break free of this fetter of forgetfulness that we arrive home because our true home exists within our minds while we inhabit this physical plane. In a world (this physical world) I was freed through another world (awareness of his consciousness within), and in an image (the illusion we humans create to give ourselves a sense of meaning and order) I was freed through a heavenly image (reality itself existing in time and space). The fetter of forgetfulness is temporary. From now on I shall rest, through the course of the time of the age, in silence (the peace and sense of meaning and purpose that comes from knowing who we really are).

David expresses a similar idea in Psalms 39:6-7 where he writes:

> "You [God] have made my days no longer than a
> hand's measure; and my years are nothing in your
> eyes; truly, every man is but a breath. Truly, every man
> goes on his way like an image; he is troubled for no
> purpose: he makes a great store of wealth, and has no
> knowledge of who will get it."

According to David, we are like hamsters on a hamster wheel going around and around collecting goods without knowing why we are collecting them. When viewed through the long-term of existence in which our life here on earth is "but a breath," our daily routines make little sense in progressing our long-term growth and knowledge. Once we are able to see through the images created by our own god leaders, the long-term picture of eternity is seen for what it is. All the running in place to achieve success in illusory structures that require the wrong focus can seem like a pointless endeavor when viewed in terms of what is really important. God comes into clear focus and suddenly the laws of the angels handed to Moses on Mt. Sinai make total sense. We realize they are the laws that prevent us from harming our own consciousness as well as the consciousness of anyone else during our sojourn on earth.

Moses' ten commandments and Jesus' consolidation of those ten commandments into two ensure the mental and emotional well-being of humanity in a natural and organic way without the intervention of god leaders like Aaron and the Sanhedrin. Breaking them to satisfy the illusion becomes non-negotiable in a conscious mind that lives for the long-term of existence. It is not hard, as the illusory systems and human god leaders would have us believe, once we realize it is the only means we have for steering a life existing in time and space in the right direction while it inhabits a physical body that may be tempted to follow a different set of rules for purposes of its own survival.

The difficulty arises when societies become like the one Stephen and Jesus were in. When the human god leaders do not allow their subordinates any means for survival other than through total conformance to them and their systems of governance, then it can become nearly impossible to live a real life without suffering some serious physical, economic, social, and/or emotional consequences. That is why Jesus said he will rest through the course of the time of the age. He knew who he was and his purpose for being here. His focus on the long-term of his own existence made the Pharisees and their oppressive rules inconsequential in terms of his own soul.

Peter was a simple man, but I do not believe he was a stupid man as Caiaphas and his colleagues took him for due to his lack of education. (Acts 4:13) Knowing his environment, particularly after witnessing what happened to Jesus, it is quite likely that Peter decided to take a more pragmatic approach that changed the message but kept him safe. It would have been far better for everyone if he had gone back to fishing because changing the message effectively destroyed the message and put his soul and the souls of his followers in the same boat they were in before Jesus showed up. They remained in their sin because they remained in their ignorance.

2
Peter And Paul Make A Deal

Peter Hands The Mantle To Paul

When Peter appears before the Sanhedrin, he is preaching that Jesus grants Israel repentance and forgiveness of sins through the holy Spirit that is given to those who obey God. (Acts 5:31-32) His statement infuriates the chief priests to the point that they want to kill him until Gamaliel steps in and tells them how it works to their advantage.

While Peter is testifying before the Sanhedrin, Paul while he was still known as Saul, was working for the Council by imprisoning and killing the followers of Jesus. He had not yet traveled on the road to Damascas where he claimed to have had his miraculous conversion. Therefore, Peter's testimony before the Sanhedrin shows that he is the inventor of the holy Spirit doctrine that Paul later ran with to expand his churches. Without Peter, I do not believe there ever would have been a Paul.

As far as we know, the first time the two men encounter one another is in Jerusalem. According to the history provided in the Book of Acts, Paul preaches for a long time in Damascus after his conversion on the road to Damascus. When he finally decides to meet with the twelve apostles in Jerusalem, they want nothing to do with him because his reputation as a killer of the followers of Jesus has preceded him. Although they are scared of him, the apostles do eventually agree to meet with Paul after their trusted colleague, Barnabas, vouches for him. However, it appears that the apostles never gain the same level of trust in Paul as Barnabas has because it only takes a single argument with the Hellenists for them to find an excuse for getting rid of Paul by sending him back to his hometown of Tarsus. (See Acts 9:19-30)

Paul is back in Tarsus working as a tent maker when Peter is summoned by a Gentile named Cornelius to meet with him. It was against Jewish law for Jews to mix with Gentiles but when Peter is asked to meet with this rich, Gentile centurian who has been very generous with his alms giving to Jews in the past; Peter cannot pass up the opportunity. (Acts 10:2) Peter is well aware of the law prohibiting him from mingling with Gentiles and it appears that he was worried about it during his entire trip to see Cornelius because in Acts 10:9, we are told he begins praying about it before having lunch with his generous donor. Miraculously, all his worries are resolved by a vision he has during his prayer. The passage in Acts 10:10-22 describes how Peter falls into a trance whereby he sees a large white sheet descending from heaven which contains all the birds and four-legged animals on earth. A voice from the sheet tells him, "Get up, Peter. Slaughter and eat." When he protests saying that nothing profane has ever entered his mouth, the voice repeats three times that what God has made clean he is not to call profane. Peter then goes to lunch with Cornelius and his family and they are all baptized after hearing Peter speak. It turns out to be a very successful trip where many Gentiles are baptized.

Riding high after his successful meeting with Cornelius, Peter is swiftly brought back to reality upon his return to Jerusalem. His circumcised Jewish colleagues are not at all happy with him for breaking the law to meet with and baptize the uncircumcised Gentiles. In his own defense, Peter tells them about the vision he had of the blanket filled with animals and birds descending from heaven with instructions that he is to eat the meat of slaughtered animals. He tells them his interpretation of the dream as meaning that God views the Gentiles as human just like the Jews; therefore, if God deems him worthy to receive the holy Spirit then there is no reason why the Gentiles should not be given the same opportunity. The Jews understand the inherent logic in that statement without bothering to question the theology of it and they quit their complaining after concluding that "God has then granted life-giving repentance to the Gentiles too." (Acts 11:1-18)

Peter was no doubt relieved at their agreement with him. However, I cannot help but believe that no matter how Peter justified it, the eating of meat that had never before touched his mouth must have been nauseating – not only for his digestive organs but for his spiritual organs as well. It is therefore not surprising that in the very next chapter of Acts, we meet up with Paul again after he is summoned back from Tarsus. Apparently, while Peter was making his foray into the Gentile world, the Jews who scattered after the persecution following Stephen's killing had all settled in Phoenicia, Cyprus and Antioch and were "preaching the word to no one but Jews." (Acts 11:19) Some among them, however, began preaching to the Greeks in Antioch proclaiming the Lord Jesus. Word of these preachers reached the ears of the Jerusalem church, of which Peter was head, and they sent Barnabus to Antioch to check it out. (Acts 11:22)

When Barnabas sees the great strides being made in Antioch bringing large numbers of people to the Lord, he goes to Tarsus and brings Paul back with him to Antioch. "And they were with the church there for a year, teaching the people; and the disciples were first given the name of Christians in Antioch." (Acts 11:26)

One can certainly assume that Barnabas would not of his own volition sought out a man who was banished by the apostles and then work with him for a year in a ministry in Antioch. Barnabas would have needed the permission of the church, and in particular the permission of Peter as its head, in order to work with a man they unapologetically and unceremoniously sent packing back to Tarsus.

Although I can safely make that assumption, it is Paul himself who provides the proof. Keeping in mind that Peter was head of the Jerusalem church comprised of Jews and keeping in mind that Peter had to break with Jewish law to retrieve a donation from Cornelius the Gentile and keeping in mind that he also had to break with Jewish tradition and custom to do it; then the following passage from Galatians 2:7-10 wherein Paul is describing a meeting that took place at the Council of Jerusalem makes perfect sense:

> "When they saw that I had been made responsible for preaching the good news to those without circumcision, even as Peter had been for those of the circumcision (Because he who was working in Peter as the Apostle of the circumcision was working no

less in me among the Gentiles); When they saw the grace which was given to me, James and Cephas and John, who had the name of being pillars, gave to me and Barnabas their right hands as friends so that we might go to the Gentiles, and they to the circumcision; Only it was their desire that we would give thought to the poor; which very thing I had much in mind to do."

According to these verses, Paul and Barnabas were put in charge of the uncircumcised Gentiles while Peter, aka Cephas, John and James remained in charge of the circumcised Jews. The only plausible time when this split in ministry between the circumcised Jews and the uncircumcised Gentiles could have taken place was in Antioch when Barnabas brought Paul back into the fold. The passage below indicates that Peter was in Antioch at the time Paul was called back and it makes it abundantly clear how averse Peter was to mixing with the uncircumcised Gentiles:

Galatians 2:11-14: "But when Cephas [Peter] came to Antioch, I made a protest against him to his face, because he was clearly in the wrong. For before certain men came from James, he did take food with the Gentiles: but when they came, he went back and made himself separate, fearing those who were of the circumcision. And the rest of the Jews went after him, so that even Barnabas was overcome by their false ways. But when I saw that they were not living uprightly in agreement with the true words of the good news, I said to Cephas [Peter] before them all, If you, being a Jew, are living like the Gentiles, and not like the Jews, how will you make the Gentiles do the same as the Jews?"

Paul definitely has a point here. Peter didn't want to associate with the uncircumcised Gentiles out of fear of what the circumcised Jews would think of him. That is probably why Peter had Barnabas bring Paul back. Peter wanted out but Paul didn't see it that way. He viewed Peter as a hypocrite for wanting to convert Gentiles by fitting in with them, while at the same time, changing his habits when Jews were around. What Paul was saying is true. Peter was a hypocrite who didn't want to deal with the hypocrisy anymore. He wanted to pass the mantle on to Paul so that he would no longer have to play the game of pretending to be something he wasn't.

Paul did not have the same internal conflict as Peter. He had no trouble telling the Gentiles they did not have to follow Jewish law even though he himself remained a devout Pharisaic Jew his entire life. (Acts 23:6, Acts 25:5) I didn't understand this disconnect until I realized that nowhere in any of his letters does Paul refer to himself as anything other than a devout Jew and follower of the law. He viewed the uncircumcised Gentiles as uncircumcised Gentiles and the circumcised Jews as circumcised Jews. They were two distinct groups of people that required a distinct doctrine. That is why he could tell the Gentiles they did not have to follow any of the Mosaic laws to be followers of Christ while at the same time, he remained a devout Jew who never missed making it to a holy event in Jerusalem. (Acts 19:16)

Paul was the consummate politician and legal tactician who could compartmentalize his ethical principles depending upon the audience he was addressing. He was a man for all seasons. He says it himself in 1 Corinthians 9:19-23:

"I have made myself a slave to all so as to win over as

many as possible. To the Jews I became like a Jew to win over Jews; to those under the law I became like one under the law—though I myself am not under the law—to win over those under the law. To those outside the law I became like one outside the law—though I am not outside God's law but within the law of Christ—to win over those outside the law. To the weak I became weak, to win over the weak. <u>I have become all things to all, to save at least some</u>. All this I do for the sake of the gospel, so that I too may have a share in it."

If speaking to Jews in the synagogue or defending himself in court, Paul was a devout follower of Mosaic law. If speaking to Gentiles, the law didn't matter. If he had to say he was something he wasn't, then it was a good thing because it won him more followers to fill his churches. People who say one thing for public consumption and do another in their personal lives are hypocrites. I think I can say unequivocally that Paul was the real hypocrite. He was a political animal who said one thing for the consumption of the public he was trying to influence and upon whom he depended for his financial livelihood and did another thing in private. Paul's goal was not to save Gentile souls. It was to gain followers. There is a distinct difference between the two goals and it is what separates Jesus from Paul.

Paul was not the only supposed follower of Jesus who acted so contrary to Jesus and what he taught. We already know about Peter but even James, the brother of Jesus, had no problem with compromising the truth to get a result he personally desired. Right before Paul's final trials, after which he is exiled to Rome where he eventually dies, James meets with him in Jerusalem and tells him that some of the Jewish believers who are zealous followers of the law (just like Paul, James and Peter) are very upset that Paul is telling the Jews who live among the Gentiles that they do not have to follow the laws of Moses and circumcise their children. In order to protect Paul, James tells him that they have four men who have taken a vow and that Paul should pay to have their heads shaved so that when he is seen with them it will appear that the reports about him telling Jews to abandon the law are false. "So Paul took the men, and on the next day after purifying himself together with them entered the temple to give notice of the day when the purification would be completed and the offering made for each of them." (Acts 21:15-26)

Truth was the cornerstone of Jesus' message and these men trampled on it whenever it didn't fit the story they wanted to tell. James, Peter and Paul were all turf builders willing to manipulate their environments in the pursuit of their agenda. Like many people in the massive hierarchy of the church today, these men knew how to play the system for maximum benefit. They were political animals who were more concerned with building their bases of operation than with the saving of souls. Deception and deceit of the kind Paul and James orchestrated was what Jesus spent his life combating. It was the evil Jesus wanted to eradicate from our minds and these men used it to build their churches. They trampled on Jesus and everything for which he stood. They stole his legacy not only through their false doctrine, but also through their example which has been used by many of the millions of political types who followed them both in and outside of the church.

Paul did not create the doctrine of the trinity and the holy Spirit who enters us upon our command. Peter did. However, Paul became the poster child for this doctrine. because of his successes in gaining Gentile followers who had no knowledge of Jesus or any of the Jewish prophets or scriptures. They depended upon Paul to give them their knowledge. As we will learn, Paul had no problem with twisting, turning and making up facts to fit the message. I defy anyone to find a single scripture that Paul does not misquote and/or misinterpret in his and Peter's attempt to make the Lord of the Old Testament the Jesus of the New Testament. He had to do that because when you separate God from creation - which make no mistake about it, that is exactly what they did by making the holy Spirit an object to be accepted or rejected – then that spirit has to be delivered to us by someone. Jesus became the deliverer of the holy Spirit who then delivers us from sin.

Paul's Sayings Indicate He Knew The Living Jesus In The Flesh

How did it happen that the belief system of the man upon which Christianity says it is based become completely unrecognizable in the hands of Paul? Any objective analysis of Paul is difficult, as it is with all chameleon personality types who readily adapt their opinions and beliefs to those required by the circumstances at hand. They are like moving targets you can never pin down. Trying to pin down Paul's actual belief system is an extremely difficult exercise because it changed from one moment to the next depending upon who his target audience was and what his external circumstances required of him. As he himself proudly admitted, he was all things to all people.

All we have are Paul's letters and they are written by him. Even though he puts himself in the best possible light of being a tireless fighter for the cause, his manipulations and deceit are on full display for anyone who is willing to read them objectively without fear of being labeled a heretic or worse. Although Christianity has used Paul's self-proclamations of hardships and imprisonments to prove he is the real deal, when one reads these proclamations in the context of his actual writings, they are always used by Paul to manipulate his followers into believing what he is saying is true even though what he is saying has little correlation to what Jesus said.

I struggled so long and so hard in coming to an understanding of Paul. It required me to understand the patterns of human consciousness that allow most of us to believe we are good and honest people even if we never question ourselves or the facts.

I believe the reason Paul did not feel he needed to talk to or even meet with the apostles of Jesus for a long time after his conversion is because in his mind he knew just as much as they did from the countless hours he spent stalking Jesus with his fellow Pharisees in order to entrap him. I go into a great amount of detail in my book, *The Mobbing of Jesus Christ*, about how the Pharisees constantly harassed Jesus in their attempts to get him arrested on a charge of blasphemy. They followed him everywhere asking him questions meant to make him slip and say something he shouldn't. Paul describes using these same harassment techniques against the followers of Jesus in the passage below:

> Acts 26:9-11: "I myself once thought that I had to do many things against the name of Jesus the Nazorean, and I did so in Jerusalem. I imprisoned many of the holy ones with the authorization I received from the chief priests, and when they were to be put to death I cast my vote against them. Many times, in synagogue after synagogue, I punished them in an attempt to

<u>force them to blaspheme;</u> I was so enraged against them that I pursued them even to foreign cities."

Paul was a murderer doing the bidding of the chief priests. He says he punished the followers of Jesus in an attempt to get them to blaspheme. I think we can safely change "punished" to "tortured." He says he was so enraged at them that he pursued them from city to city. What would cause Paul to become enraged at people who have done him no wrong – to the point that he would torture them so he could arrest them based on false confessions? What causes any person or regime to punish, torture and imprison people who have done them no harm? What is it within us as human beings that we can get so filled with hate towards certain people because they disagree with us? What is it that threatens certain people like Paul so much that they become enraged and stalk people from city to city? I don't have the answers to these questions. However, I think we must find the answers because it is a human trait that is still with us and is causing many innocent people to be stalked and hounded because they hold certain beliefs that are contrary to those of people like Paul and the chief priests who are willing to punish them for those beliefs.

As the one receiving the authorization of the chief priests to capture, torture and imprison the followers of Jesus, Paul must have been an expert at his job. He had to have learned his craft somewhere. I think he learned it in the many hours he spent with his fellow Pharisees tracking down and harassing Jesus from city to city. We mustn't forget that Jesus and Paul were the same age and contemporaries of one another.[8] Being that they were both the same age and both studied the law, it could be that they knew one another quite well. Although Paul claims never to have met the living Jesus, his own use of many of Jesus's actual words and sayings indicate otherwise. One or two instances could be explained as coincidence or a paraphrase of something he heard the apostles say, but when you look at them in their totality, it becomes apparent that not only did Paul lift them off the living Jesus, he also changes their meaning to make them fit his altered and oftentimes confusing paradigm.

Jesus' Sayings Butchered by Paul

Jesus: *"Let your 'Yes' mean 'Yes,' and your 'No' mean 'No.'* Anything more is from the evil one." (Matthew 5:37)

Paul: "So when I intended this, did I act lightly? Or do I make my plans according to human considerations, so that with me *it is "yes, yes" and "no, no"*? (2 Corinthians 1:17)

Jesus: "Early in the morning, as they were walking along, they saw the fig tree withered to its roots. Peter remembered and said to him, "Rabbi, look! The fig tree that you cursed has withered." Jesus said to them in reply, "Have faith in God. Amen, *I say to you, whoever says to this mountain, 'Be lifted up and thrown into the sea,' and does not doubt in his heart but believes that what he says will happen, it shall be done for him.* Therefore I tell you, all that you ask for in prayer, believe that you will receive it and it shall be yours." (Mark 11:20-24)

Paul: "If I speak in human and angelic tongues but do not have love, I am a resounding gong or a clashing cymbal. And if I have the gift of prophecy and comprehend all mysteries and all knowledge; *if I have all faith so as to move mountains* but do not have love, I am nothing." (1 Corinthians 13:1-2)

Jesus: *"You are the salt of the earth. But if salt loses its taste, with what can* *it be seasoned? It is no longer good for anything but to be thrown out and trampled underfoot.* " (Matthew 5:13)

Paul: "Let your speech always be gracious, *seasoned with salt*, so that you know how you should respond to each one." (Colossians 4:6)

Jesus: *"Therefore, stay awake! For you do not know on which day your Lord will come. Be sure of this: if the master of the house had known the hour of night when the thief was coming, he would have stayed awake and not let his house be broken into.* So too, you also must be prepared, for at an hour you do not expect, the Son of Man will come." (Matthew 24:42-44)

Paul: "Concerning times and seasons, brothers, you have no need for anything to be written to you. *For you yourselves know very well that the day of the Lord will come like a thief at night.* When people are saying, "Peace and security," then sudden disaster comes upon them, like labor pains upon a pregnant woman, and they will not escape."   (1 Thessalonians 5:1-3)

Jesus: *"The kingdom of heaven is like unto leaven, which a woman took, and hid in three measures of meal, till the whole was leavened."* (Matthew 13:33)

Paul: "Your boasting is not appropriate. *Do you not know that a little yeast leavens all the dough? Clear out the old yeast, so that you may become a fresh batch of dough, inasmuch as you are unleavened.* For our paschal lamb, Christ, has been sacrificed. Therefore let us celebrate the feast, not with the old yeast, the yeast of malice and wickedness, but with the unleavened bread of sincerity and truth." (1 Corinthians 5:6-7)

"You were running well; who hindered you from following [the] truth? That enticement does not come from the one who called you. *A little yeast leavens the whole batch of dough.* I am confident of you in the Lord that you will not take a different view, and that the one who is troubling you will bear the condemnation, whoever he may be. As for me, brothers, if I am still preaching circumcision, why am I still being persecuted? In that case, the stumbling block of the cross has been abolished. Would that those who are upsetting you might also castrate themselves!" (Galatians 5:7-12)

Everything Jesus says has profound meaning with regard to self knowledge and awareness as the pathway to God within. Paul takes these sacred instructions and turns them into mush. However, I'll give him the benefit of the doubt. If Paul was in the crowds listening to Jesus, the message may have touched him, but he just didn't have the wherewithal or practical experience to interpret it properly. Jesus was delivering a revolutionary message that would have gotten him arrested on the spot if articulated in a way that made a Pharisee like Paul understand it. It was blasphemous to view God as anything other than the all-powerful, all-seeing and all-knowing guy in the sky who is separate and apart from his creation.

Jesus was trying to say that God is the consciousness within all of us that directs our growth – both our mental and our physical growth. God is all-powerful, all-seeing and all-knowing not because he is looking down on us from in heaven, but because God is us. The kingdom of God is one with us like the yeast is to the dough to make it rise for baking. Separating God's consciousness from our own is as impossible as separating yeast from the dough. It cannot be done and when authoritarians like Paul, James and Peter try it, our mental and emotional growth becomes stagnant, depressed, resigned and even dangerous depending upon the kinds of beliefs and rules they are pushing us to adopt to replace it.

Jesus's metaphors may have been lost on Paul because he had no frame of reference for them. His consciousness of God had long ago been replaced with the laws of Moses and the murderous belief system of the Pharisee hierarchy he was climbing. Maybe his intent to redefine Jesus' words was not based in malicious intent as much as it was in ignorance. He could have been like me when I was a young adult going through some turmoil in my life. By that time, I had left the Baptist church of my youth. I don't think I ever read the Bible while going to church except for the verses that were posted in the weekly bulletin received during Sunday service. I turned to the Bible to seek some answers during my difficulties and while reading the Gospels of Jesus, I was amazed at Jesus's parables. Although I didn't know what they all meant at the time, they convinced me that Jesus was probably the most exceptional person I had ever encountered in person or in print. It was a visceral connection that unfortunately did not make any substantive change in my mind or my situation at that time. It was not until I opened the book again some 30 years later that I was able to read those same parables with the proper context; after having read other books and texts in my effort to recover from a workplace trauma. It was from that experience and the incredible toll it took on my mind that I was able to see that the real part of me is my consciousness of what is right and what is wrong in terms of the way my actions, words and beliefs affect other people as well as myself. If I had not made myself put my mind in the minds of the people who harmed me in order to understand their motivations for doing what they did to me, I never would have come to an understanding of my own motivations and the role my own ego and naivete played in my suffering. Once my eyes were opened in this way, Jesus' message of the kingdom of God being within made all the sense in the world to me and it opened the knowledge of the ages contained in the entire

Bible to me. I became one of the blind who could finally see. Instead of having my own experience consume my mind 24/7, my mind expanded out to recognizing similar abuses of the human mind experienced by people everywhere. I found my own humanity after metaphorically getting hit over the head by people who had lost theirs to all the same things I had lost mine to.

Paul, while he was still Saul, had lost his humanity to a Pharisee hierarchy which had lost its consciousness of life. In Matthew 23, Jesus describes them as whitewashed tombs because they had replaced their consciousness of life with values that ran counter to life, but which gave them great power, prestige and wealth within the temple structure. This loss is what allowed them to so callously destroy the lives of other people with whom they disagreed. Paul was climbing the Pharisee ladder of success by imprisoning and killing people with the same belief system as Jesus and Stephen and he was doing so with the authorization he received from the chief priests.

Paul's behavior and mindset was an asset to him as a Pharisee on the road to success. It is incredibly hard for a grown person to change habits, thoughts and beliefs acquired over a lifetime, particularly if those habits, thoughts and beliefs have helped them achieve a certain level of success and stature within the community. Paul was no different. Whether through intention or mere ignorance of what Jesus was teaching, Paul was unable to step outside the paradigm of his Pharisee upbringing to live in truth. He relied upon knowledge and strategies he was taught as a Pharisee trained at the knee of Gamaliel to build his network of churches. We all fall back on what we know if we do not acquire the knowledge, self-awareness and courage to step outside that paradigm to create a new one. Change is extremely difficult. It is a hard road for anyone to take because it requires faith in a way of life that is outside the limits of what we are familiar with and can control. Like the Israelites, most of us want to fall back on what we are familiar with even if what we are familiar with is what we want to escape from. Losing control by letting go of what is familiar to us to pursue what is right for us is terrifying, but it is the kind of faith that Jesus says we must have if we are to move mountains in a static world where conformity to what we know is an asset.

Peter And Paul Were Institution Builders

Paul's church hierarchy mirrored the temple hierarchy he was familiar with. The message of Jesus was destroyed when Peter and Paul created a message more suitable for justifying the hierarchy of church workers who would be depending upon the church for their financial sustenance. The true message of Jesus can only be applied to the individual mind. It does not lend itself well to the group think of religion. Egos build institutions like churches. A consciousness of truth like that of Jesus knows that God cannot be found in church. God can only be found in the individual mind doing the work of knowing itself. Jesus said:

> "The Realm is inside of you and outside of you. When you come to know yourselves, then you will become known, and you will realize that it is you who are the children of the living Father. But if you will not know yourselves, you live in poverty and it is you yourselves who are that poverty."[9]

Peter was a different kind of man than Jesus. He was a born

institution builder. When Jesus took James, John and Peter up on the mountain where they saw Elijah and Moses, Peter's natural reaction was to build a tent for Jesus, Elijah and Moses. (Matthew 17:4) Peter and the other disciples took Jesus literally as they usually did. After Jesus' departure, the building of a physical church became the priority and Peter became the default leader of the fledgling group of Jesus' disciples who wanted to spread his message. I believe this church building activity took priority over the message because the message that Jesus gave was only conducive to building the church of each individual soul. When you have the holy Spirit of God within yourself as your consciousness of right and wrong/true and false, there is no way that anyone else can better determine what is right and wrong for you. They can mentor, teach and guide you as Jesus did with his disciples, but they can never make decisions for you if you want to stay true to your own life force.

By using the physical structure of the temple as the example in creating a physical church, Peter defeated the purpose of the man he viewed as the Messiah. By then taking what Jesus said was the essence of our individuality - our God within – and turning it into an object that can be accepted or rejected to determine our eternal salvation, Peter did what all religious egos do for purposes of turf building. He turned Jesus's life saving message into a business and forever separated the members from any chance for salvation by misdirecting them about the meaning of repentance and salvation contained in the Old Testament.

However, Peter did not think he was doing anything wrong. He was merely doing what his ancestors had always done. From time immemorial, mankind has tried to put the consciousness of God in a box called a temple, mosque, church, etc. God cannot be put in a box because God is life itself in all its manifestations. Jesus had a life-saving message appealing to all who heard it because it brought them home to themselves. The Israelites did not have a temple or church during their forty years in the wilderness. They had the dream of a better life in the promised land and the ten commandments of consciousness that would ensure the achievement of that dream. God was the light that always preceded them because God is the light that always brings us home to ourselves while we are encased in these physical bodies on earth that need food and water to sustain themselves. It is so easy for the needs of the body to put out the light of our source and keep us from achieving what we are here to achieve. It is very tempting to build alters to God because building alters is what we do to reward our fellow men and women. Awards, accolades, monuments, names on buildings and the like are what we do to reward and recognize achievement in an ego-centered world.

How do we possibly thank a God who provides us with all we need if we follow the dictates of truth and reality in a world that thrives in secrecy and falsehoods? If we are like Solomon, we build a temple. If we are like Jesus, we live a life that reflects its source in everything we think, do and say. God does not want our monuments. Why would life have need of monuments? God does not want our money. Why would life have need of money? God created life to express itself on earth. God wants us to scream life by expressing our life force in creating what we are meant to create. That is the promised land promised to each and every one of us who has the courage to express the light of life in the darkness of a world that wants us to conform to pre-determined structures. Churches, mosques and temples do not worship God. People worship God when they live in accordance with the commandments of a human consciousness that is logical in its recognition that what harms the one harms the whole when we treat other people in ways in which we would not ourselves like to be treated.

Peter and Paul were institution builders and the Gentiles were potential customers with money to help them build their churches. I disliked both men, particularly Paul, until I realized they were men of their time. They were doing what they knew and were taught. If the conversion of the Gentiles had not become the mission of the church, Peter would never have been forced to follow a strategy of least resistance. Laws are laws, however. There are very few ways to get around them as Peter found out when he was summoned to meet with the Gentile centurian named Cornelius. Peter's vision telling him the Gentiles had as much right to the holy Spirit as anyone else was the same kind of compromising strategy of a politician who accepts a lobbyist's check under the rationalization that he can achieve so much good with the money because it will help keep him in office to pursue his particular agenda. Angels do not visit politicians telling them to accept lobbyist money, but they would if they lived in the same Pharisaic Jewish community that Peter lived in where the belief in angels and spirits was commonplace. (Acts 23:8) Our modern sensibilities do not allow for angels, so instead we are told that the lobbyist money has no influence whatsoever over the decisions our politicians make when our own spirit of truth knows differently.

Hypocrisy and deceit is a necessary evil in institution building, which is why the Pharisees were the biggest hypocrites of all. It takes money, power and influence to sustain the hierarchy of any institution. If the message you are giving is not conducive to gaining you the members whose wealth, power and influence is necessary for sustaining the institution, then the institution along with the message will never get off the ground. Any business owner knows this. In order to gain and keep customers, you must make your product a desired commodity. Marketing all too often presents spin as truth and corrupt sales tactics can turn hypocrisy (saying one thing and doing another) into profits. The subprime mortgage crisis would never have happened if every sales person who sold a home to someone who could not afford it once the interest rate rose on it would have first asked themselves if they would want to buy a home under the same set of circumstances. When the companies who employed those salesmen created the mortgages, they used the noble justification that they were putting people into homes. It was the same kind of noble justification Peter used when he said that Cornelius had just as much right to the holy Spirit as anyone else and a politician uses to justify using lobbyist money for the public good. In all cases, the people justifying their actions know the truth and they are using the justification to protect their own self interests and image.

Whenever we see deceit or hypocrisy in ourselves and others, we can be assured that our actions are wrong. Jesus railed against Pharisaic hypocrisy and deceit in Matthew 23, yet somehow we have relegated his denunciations as applying to this singular group of people. We have compartmentalized Jesus' teachings as much as we have compartmentalized our own ethics and it is this compartmentalization that keeps us from ever knowing ourselves. It makes us into shape shifters who can conform our minds to any situation while maintaining the delusion we are good people.

3
Getting To Know You

Discovering Paul

When I finished a draft of my book, *The Evolution of Good and Evil*, I had a friend tell me that Paul never met Jesus and although a contemporary of the apostles, Paul never received any teachings or training from them. That was the beginning of my study into the Pauline epistles, including the Book of Acts which provides an historical background for Paul and his message.

My own personal journey of understanding Paul was tortuous. For the greater part of the writing of this book, I hated the man who I came to view as primarily responsible for destroying the legacy of Jesus, while at the same time hiding behind the good name of Jesus to give his false teachings the credibility essential for building and maintaining his churches. Although I was never able to determine whether Paul had a malevolent motive for changing facts, distorting the message of Jesus, misquoting scripture, making up stories, appearing to be all things to all people, continuing to practice Jewish laws and traditions while telling his followers to abandon them and making money off the churches he was creating with his false doctrine; or whether he was just a weak man who could not face himself and was grabbing at straws at a redemption out of his reach, the fact remains that he falls far short of sainthood and most certainly carries the label *apostle* illicitly and without regard to his true status.

Studying Paul was an extremely difficult exercise that tested my own objectivity and ability to remain grounded in truth. Paul was a very complex and egoistic man with what we would today describe as having issues. Ironically, it was those issues that eventually helped me make peace with the man, but which created my own issues with a church that legitimized his doctrine - a doctrine that was so clearly contradictory to the Christ after whom its religion is named.

The reason I no longer have such strong feelings about what Paul did to the legacy and teachings of Jesus is because his letters provide me with all the information I need to see how false and destructive his doctrine has been to the consciousness of people who fall outside the parameters of what Paul considers moral and good conduct. The question then becomes why haven't the leaders of the Christian faith seen his letters for what they are? Why have they given the word of a man who claims to have received his doctrine from visions of a dead man the same legitimacy as the teachings of the man himself? Why were Jesus' awareness teachings hidden and/or destroyed and now that many of those teachings have been discovered, why are they not being preached instead of getting portrayed as new age evil in many cases? I address the answers to some of these questions in this book.

I now believe the New Testament of the Bible should be divided into three parts: (1) the Gospels of Jesus, (2) the false doctrine of

Paul outlined in his letters along with his endless defense against accusations he is a liar, delusional or both; and (3) the remaining short letters of Peter, James, Jude and John (including Revelation); all of which describe false teachers cleverly devising myths, an impostor apostle and many antichrists "who went out from us [the apostles] but were not really of our number." (See 2 Peter 1:16, 2 Peter 2:1-3, 1 John 2:3-5, 1 John 2:18-19, 1 John 4:2-5 and Revelation 2:2)

If people are to be truthful with themselves about the New Testament, then they need to decide if they are going to follow Jesus or Paul because their teachings are not compatible. Paul's letters undo everything Jesus tried to accomplish, which is why I believe such strong language was used to describe an antichrist who is now in the world:

> 1 John 4:2-3: "This is how you can know the Spirit of God: every spirit that acknowledges Jesus Christ come in the flesh belongs to God, and every spirit that does not acknowledge Jesus does not belong to God. This is the spirit of the antichrist that, as you heard, is to come, but in fact is already in the world."

Paul's entire doctrine came from a spirit of Jesus who Paul claimed to have heard from directly. As I write about in the rest of the book, the doctrine Paul claims to have been receiving from this spirit of Jesus bore no resemblance to the message of the living Jesus *come in the flesh*. We should ask ourselves why 'the spirit' of Jesus would have radically changed the message of Jesus in the flesh and if it was, in fact, the case that Jesus' spirit felt the need to deliver this new message, why didn't he deliver it to one of the eleven remaining disciples who were mentored by him and all whom were contemporaries of Paul?

If Joseph of Arimathea, Nicodemus and the numerous other witnesses who were silenced by Caiaphas about seeing Jesus alive are to be believed, then it would definitively prove that Paul never heard from any spirit. It would also explain the name calling and charges of false teachings the apostles were leveling against an antichrist who was not acknowledging Jesus come in the flesh and it would explain why Paul resorted to bullying tactics to silence the Corinthians and Galatians who were questioning his claims as I talk about later in the book.

Our Faith Is In Vain And We Are Still In Our Sins

Paul writes in 1 Corinthians 15:12-17:

> "Now if the good news says that Christ came back from the dead, how do some of you say that there is no coming back from the dead? But if there is no coming back from the dead, then Christ has not come back from the dead: <u>And if Christ did not come again from the dead, then our good news and your faith in it are of no effect.</u> Yes, and we are seen to be false witnesses of God; because we gave witness of God that by his power Christ came again from the dead: which is not true if there is no coming back from the dead. <u>For if it is not possible for the dead to come to life again, then Christ has not come to life again: And if that is so, your faith is of no effect; you are still in your sins.</u>"

Whether or not Jesus actually rose from the dead in the flesh has become an important bone of contention in the age of reason where the church has found itself bleeding members at record numbers. In Paul's own words in 1 Corinthians 15, Christianity rises or falls around the truth of it. The modern church cannot change this central doctrine without facing the risk of watching its worldwide religious hierarchy of workers, money and power come to a crashing halt because they have all been false witnesses to God for 2,000+ years. Since the church has decided it cannot change this central doctrine without destroying itself, it is left with a couple of options that all business institutions have when they face the prospect of extinction. It can use re-branding techniques to make subtle changes to this very clear statement of Paul's through a change in its advertising to where it becomes a metaphysical resurrection of the soul rather than an actual raising of the dead in the flesh; or it can discontinue this product line of doctrine entirely by focusing on other aspects of the religion that are more palatable to an educated and informed public and then recruit charismatic leaders to sell the new and improved message.

There is a third option that the church has refused to consider from its earliest beginnings at the Council of Jerusalem in 50 A.D. and later at the First Council of Nicaea in 325 A.D. Tell the truth. Simply open the vaults and provide a means for all the information to be made available to the public without labeling it heresy, unreliable, forgery and fake. Let the audience members the church is supposedly serving decide for themselves what Jesus wanted them to know. There is no greater gift that a person can receive than the truth. It is truth, not love, that covers a multitude of sins.

Absent the church providing the world with the third option, the only means for determining the truth for ourselves is to analyze the material currently available to us with a mind willing to consider possibilities other than the ones that have been spoon fed to us by our religious institutions. Freeing myself from the sainthood aspect of Paul allowed me to see the human being. It allowed me to question the assumptions underlying his conclusions. It allowed me to see the lunacy in all his if-then statements where his conclusions (then statements) have no relationship to the facts he lays out (if statements) and the facts he lays out have no relationship to the truth. It opened my heart to the bitterness and resentment underlying his name calling of the apostles. It opened my eyes to the bullying methods he used to get his churches to conform to a message that made as little sense to them as it did to me as a child and young adult. It allowed me to ask basic questions like the church at Corinth was asking Paul. For instance, why does it matter if Jesus came back from the dead in the flesh or not? How does that one fact make him the Messiah? Why did Paul make this an article of faith upon which our eternal salvation rests? What does having that faith do for us anyway? What substantive, qualitative changes occur in people's lives because they have declared belief that a man rose from the dead so that he can now live in their hearts?

There is no way we can ever prove conclusively that Jesus did not die on the cross, but the laws of physics and science have proven unequivocally that a physical body once dead does not come back to life. If it does, then it was not dead to begin with. Just because a physical body is resuscitated after losing bodily function, as happens in NDE cases, does not make it the foundation for a claim that the person is God so that a religion can be created based on that foundation. Even still, Paul made resurrection the foundation upon which it all falls if people do not believe. They do not believe and are leaving the church in droves. So now the physical resurrection of Christ is being preached more and more with a metaphysical interpretation of renewal and hope. However, all such preaching is hypocritical. Paul makes it abundantly clear that we have to believe in a physical resurrection in order to have faith in God. If not, we are still in our sin.

If it turns out Jesus never died, the Christianity of Paul and the massive church hierarchy his doctrine created would fall like a house of cards. The truth that Caiaphas and Pilate tried so hard to keep hidden would finally be revealed and the consciousness-raising teachings of Jesus that have been co-opted by other people and manipulated to serve their agendas will regain their rightful place as the creation of the mind of the Messiah who made it his mission to help us apply their lessons to our own minds.

4
Beware The False Prophets

Why Does Paul Leave Out The Why Of His Conversion?

Peter's holy Spirit compromise to the message of Jesus condemned Paul to the hell that Jesus the Messiah was sent to free us from and Paul, in turn, condemned all the Gentiles he was charged with converting. I hated Paul for so long because I thought he was malevolent. I was wrong. He was just weak – too weak to face down the strong ego that led him in such a wrong direction but had brought him so much adulation in the Pharisaic community. When he failed to achieve the same adulation from the apostles in the Christian community, that same strong ego made him very bitter and resentful towards them.

The process of knowing ourselves involves asking ourselves why we do what we do and think what we think. Jesus' entire philosophy is based on this means of determining the motive for our behavior by determining the state of our individual minds. Jesus said,

> Matthew 12:33-37: "Either declare the tree good and
> its fruit good, or declare the tree rotten and its fruit

rotten, for a tree is known by its fruit. How can you
say good things when you are evil? For from the
fullness of the heart the mouth speaks. A good
person brings forth good out of a store of goodness
but an evil person brings forth evil out of a store of
evil. I tell you, on the day of judgment people will
render an account for every careless word they speak.
By your words you will be acquitted and by your
words you will be condemned."

We have no way of knowing if we are bringing forth good or evil
if we never bother to analyze ourselves. If we never take the time
for determining our motives for doing what we do or saying what
we say, we can easily fall victim to our own ego's rationalizations,
justifications and agendas. It was acceptable for Paul to kill the
followers of Jesus in the community of people he was in. He was, in
fact, on his way to Damascus to imprison and kill the followers of
Jesus when he had his miraculous conversion. Other than the story
Paul tells about hearing the voice of Jesus, we know next to nothing
about Paul's motivation for converting. What was the trigger for his
conversion? What was it that made him want to make a radical
change in his life? Why did he choose to give up a way of life that
brought him so much adulation from powerful people to one of a
disciple who would have been spurned by those same people? I
think I find the absence of an explanation for Paul's conversion to
be the strangest aspect of his letters – that he gives us so little in
terms of his own personal motivation for making such a radical
change in his mind and life, if indeed such a radical change actually
took place. Given the extent of the information we have at hand, it
is hard to tell.

Why would someone leave the 'why' out of the equation? I think in Paul's case, it may have been due to his personal inability to ask it of himself. He was a man who was unaware that he was unaware but instinctively knew that if he began asking why in order to become aware, it would open up a Pandora's box of thoughts and emotions he would be unable to deal with under the light of truth. I think that is the reason why he cloaked his murders behind the rationalization that he committed them while under the law. It also could have been why he never apologized for them. It takes inner strength to admit we are wrong, particularly when we want to remain in the good graces of a community of people who believe what we did was right.

Paul was not a stupid man. He knew the true message of Jesus because he killed people like Stephen for preaching it. He also knew that if he was to embrace the true message, it would result in punishment in the physical world and it would definitely cause turmoil in his inner world. He wanted to avoid both eventualities and ironically in his avoidance, he suffered terrible physical punishment and constant inner turmoil that he described as Satan's thorns in the following passage:

> "'Therefore, that I might not become too elated, a thorn in the flesh was given to me, an angel of Satan, to beat me, to keep me from being too elated. Three times I begged the Lord about this, that it might leave me, but he said to me, "My grace is sufficient for you, for power is made perfect in weakness." I will rather boast most gladly of my weaknesses in order that the power of Christ may dwell with me. Therefore, I am content with weaknesses, insults, hardships, persecutions, and constraints, for the sake of Christ;

for when I am weak, then I am strong.[10]

This sounds like a man doing his own form of repentance because no person is strong when they are weak. It is impossible to be strong while in a state of weakness just as it is impossible for Paul to confess his guilt by apologizing for the imprisonment and killing of innocent followers of Jesus like Stephen. By avoiding true repentance through self-examination, Paul never dealt with his guilt and although he admits to his crimes in his letters, he never expresses any remorse for them, nor does he offer any apology to either his victims or their families. Instead, he rationalizes them by always saying he committed his crimes while under the law. He even goes one step further, and makes this the justification for giving up the law entirely; including the law of the angels Moses brought down the mountain.

The ten commandments of consciousness that Moses brought down the mountain are both defensive and offensive laws of the human mind. They are excellent rules that keep us internally focused. They do not allow for an ego that requires constant nourishment from other people and environments where reputations become an essential requirement for success. With these commandments as his guide, Paul would never have sought adulation from his superiors by killing his fellow men and women. If he had loved his own life force [God within] with all his heart, mind, body and soul, he would have nurtured it by loving it in other people. He would have apologized to the families of the good men and women he killed and imprisoned. All the time he served in prison that he was always so quick to point to as a symbol of how hard he worked for the cause would have actually served a purpose.

He could have used that time to pay true penance for the damage he did to the consciousness of so many innocent men and women.

Paul's Damascus Conversion Is More Vacuous Than It Is Miraculous

Our perspective needs to get switched when it comes to viewing Paul's miraculous conversion on the road to Damascus. According to the account found in Acts 9:1-30, Saul/Paul is commissioned by the high priest to go to Damascus and bring back in chains any followers of Jesus. While traveling to Damascus, Saul is blinded by a bright light and hears a voice asking him, "Saul, Saul, why are you persecuting me?" When Paul asks, "Who are you, sir,?"the reply is, "I am Jesus, whom you are persecuting. Now get up and go into the city and you will be told what you must do. The men who were traveling with him stood speechless, for they heard the voice but could see no one."

The church has taken Paul's version of events on face value and has built a doctrine around a man who claims to have received his theology from the vision and voice of a dead Jesus. I believe Paul's story could be another example of what came first, the chicken or the egg. What if instead of believing that Paul heard from the spirit of Jesus, we ask ourselves if this story might have been invented after a less miraculous conversion took place in order to give credibility to a person who was preaching about   a holy Spirit that enters our hearts and teaches us how to do good?

I would suggest that the conversion story was embellished after the fact for purposes of reinforcing Paul's claim that he received his doctrine directly from the 'risen' savior, rather than from Jesus himself. One of the strongest pieces of evidence for this embellishment theory is the fact that Paul changes his story.

Something as important as a conversion that changes the trajectory of a person's life, particularly if it happens in as spectacular a way as Paul claims, does not render itself to versions. Every detail of an event like Paul claims to have experienced would have been seared into his mind, yet that is not the case with Paul.

The description of Saul's conversion on the road to Damascus is given to us in Acts, Chapter 9. In that version of events, the men who were traveling with Saul/Paul stood speechless because they heard the voice [of Jesus] but could not see anyone. Paul later changes this witness detail when he is defending himself in court against some Jerusalem Jews who are accusing him of "teaching everyone everywhere against the people and the law and this place, and what is more, he has even brought Greeks into the temple and defiled this sacred place." (Acts 21:27-28) After stating that he himself is a Jew, strictly educated in the law at the feet of Gamaliel, Paul tells them about his conversion on the road to Damascus, only this time he says, "My companions saw the light, but did not hear the voice of the one who spoke to me." (Acts 22:9)

Many experts in theology will argue that this was an error in translation and they are entitled to their opinions. However, I think this change in events makes perfect sense when one realizes that Paul wanted to set himself up as the divine receiver of the word of Christ [and tangentially God after making Jesus the son of God]. His original version of events did not make him the sole gatekeeper to God's will if other people are hearing the same voice he is hearing. He has to revise his original version of the conversion if he is to retain his position as the sole conduit to God. That way he retains total control over the message he gives to the members of his churches.

As a Pharisee preaching to an audience of Pharisees and Jews, hearing from the spirit of Jesus would have bolstered the message rather than hinder it because of the Pharisee belief in angels, spirits and miracles. (Acts 23:8) Where Paul began to run into problems was with his Gentile audience who did not put as much stock into angels and visions as the Pharisees did. As I discuss later in the book, Paul had to use the indoctrination tactics of the Bully/Bystander/Enabler/Target Model of behavior I identify in my book, *The Evolution of Good and Evil,* to force feed them the message when they began doubting his claims. These techniques have been used ever since by a Christian hierarchy who finds that the kind of honesty and transparency that Jesus and Stephen shepherded can oftentimes be detrimental to its financial health. Demotions, excommunications, terminations, banishment, shaming, arrests, imprisonments and even executions have all been a part and continue to be a part of Christian history, as they are of all religious history when the myth of God as the guy in the sky begins to be exposed as religion's true form of heresy.

The Evolution of the Law in Paul's Doctrine

Paul's conversion presents problems on several fronts. What is it exactly he was converted to? He remained a devout Jew while preaching his holy Spirit doctrine to Gentiles. It is important to note that Peter remained a Jew as well and Jesus was never anything but a Jew. The "Christian" moniker that was given to the Gentile followers at Antioch seems to be a label that was exclusively meant for them. They were singled out as a specific group by Paul and then more formally at the Council of Jerusalem by James and Peter, as I will explain a bit later.

The Gentiles were customers for a holy Spirit religion that was unknown to Jews and which failed to convert even its founders. James, Peter, John and Paul all remained Jewish. Why wouldn't the founders of a movement want to adopt its beliefs? Why wouldn't a company owner endorse its product by using it personally? Why wouldn't a polluter want to drink the water he claims is safe for other people to drink? Usually the answer to those questions is that what is good for the goose is not good for the gander. People who would foist a belief system on other people that they themselves do not believe look at their target audience as just that: targets. The Gentiles were non-Jews who were easy targets for a highway to heaven doctrine that required little of them, other than money for the collection plate. Paul not only abandoned the 600+ laws of Moses to attract them, he also abandoned the Ten Commandments. The only requirement for salvation? Ask for the holy Spirit of Jesus to come into your heart and you are good to go.

In his quest to pander to his audience of Gentiles, Paul eventually refers to the Ten Commandments as the ministry of death, but it took an evolution in his doctrine to get there. After Paul's conversion and before he leaves Damascus to join the apostles in Jerusalem, the Bible only says that Paul "began at once to proclaim Jesus in the synagogues, that he is the Son of God." (Acts 9:20-25) That is the extent of his doctrine right after his conversion and before he meets with Peter and the other apostles during his first trip to Jerusalem. There is no mention of the holy Spirit or the forgiveness of sins through Jesus.

When Barnabas brings Paul back from Tarsus after he has been banished there by the apostles after his argument with the Hellenists, Acts 11:26 says that the two of them spend a year in Antioch working with the church and that it is there that the disciples are first called Christians. I think this may be the most profound verse in the Bible in terms of the course change in human thought it signifies. It is in Antioch where Paul completely abandons the people he claims to be saving. He consciously replaces the teachings of Jesus with the myth of a holy Spirit that is given to converts from God through the spirit of Jesus with the assistance of the church and its facilitators. Paul brought the same false hierarchical model of the Jewish temple into his new Christian churches. Under this structure, the guy in the sky god who is all powerful gives Jesus the task of distributing the holy Spirit to people who profess a belief in him. This transfer of spirit is facilitated through God's intermediaries on earth who pledge loyalty to Jesus by dedicating themselves to the work of the church. The priests, bishops and deacons become the earthly gatekeepers to God through Jesus. The model would look something like this:

Paul's Hierarchy of Salvation

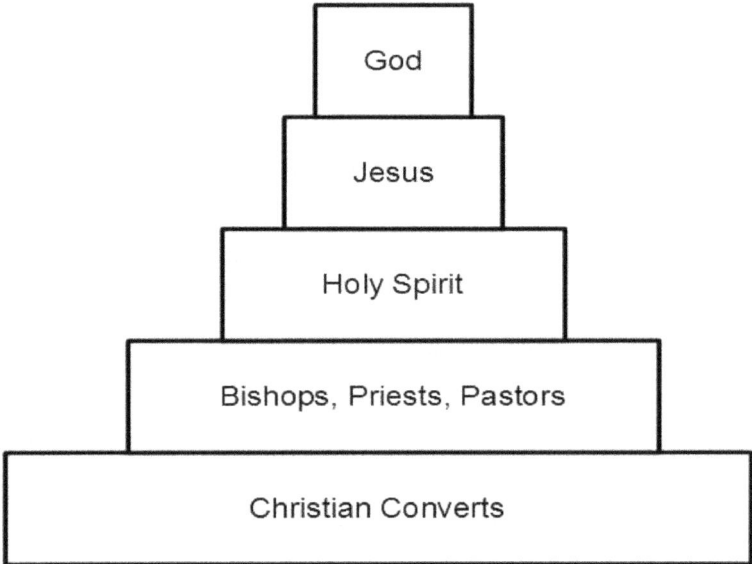

Christians like to call this course change the "New Covenant" as opposed to the "Old Covenant" of the Old Testament. I suppose it could be aptly described as a new covenant if by new covenant is meant a complete split with the truth. The kingdom of God that Jesus explains to Nicodemus in John, Chapter 3, can only be found within the individual human mind becomes five degrees separated from us in Paul's theology. In Paul's hierarchy, God gives his spirit to the spirit of Jesus who then passes it on to the people asking for it through an army of church workers who act as intermediaries.

After what I have concluded was a strategy session that took place between Paul and Peter during Peter's visit to Antioch, Barnabas and Paul eventually set out from Antioch on their first mission trip. This trip is where Paul articulates the doctrine of abandoning all the laws of Moses in favor of the salvation the holy Spirit provides. Acts 13:44-46 says that almost the whole city gathered together to hear the "word of the Lord" delivered by Paul and Barnabus, but that not everyone who came to hear them was happy with what they were hearing. The Jews in the city became absolutely incensed with them, but were unsuccessful in stopping them and Paul's gospel spread through the region with the promise of eternal life it provided to all by a simple declaration of believing in the holy Spirit. (Acts 13:48-49)

Under Paul's doctrine of the Holy Trinity, God the Father gives a person the holy Spirit through his son Jesus Christ who came down from heaven to serve as a human sacrifice for the sins of mankind to those who accept this as truth. Paul fully expresses this doctrine in Titus 3:3-8, where he says:

> "For we ourselves were once foolish, disobedient, deluded, slaves to various desires and pleasures, living in malice and envy, hateful ourselves and hating one another. But when the kindness and generous love of God our savior appeared, not because of any righteous deeds we had done but because of his mercy, he saved us through the bath of rebirth and renewal by the holy Spirit,whom he richly poured out on us through Jesus Christ our savior, so that we might be justified by his grace and become heirs in hope of eternal life."

Then immediately following this passage in verse 9, Paul says, "This saying is trustworthy." This is one of seven times when Paul has to write that he is not lying – that what he is saying is trustworthy. (See Galatians 1:20, 1 Timothy 2:7, 1 Timothy 1:15, 1 Timothy 3:1, 1 Timothy 4:9 and Titus 3:8) Paul had to back up this passage with one of his 'I'm not lying' assurances because the idea of a triune god was something that neither the Gentiles nor the Jews had ever heard before; either from Jesus, the Pharisees or even Peter for that matter. This was all Paul's ideology. Paul made Jesus a god. There is nothing of Jesus' teachings in Paul's doctrine. Paul made it all about this mythical god/man who descended from heaven to die for our sins. In Paul's convoluted storyline, one man (Jesus) came from heaven to cancel out the sin of one man (Adam). Mankind was condemned by the sin of one physical man, therefore Paul reasoned, mankind could be redeemed by one physical man:

> Romans 5:17: "For, if by the wrongdoing of one, death was ruling through the one, much more will those to whom has come the wealth of grace and the giving of righteousness, be ruling in life through the one, even Jesus Christ."

Paul wanted one man's death to atone for all sin – past, present and future. The message wouldn't work in gaining followers if it was interpreted as one salvation for one sin. So Paul says that Adam's transgression in the Garden condemned all men and women thereafter. He had to make this claim in order to have the death and resurrection of Jesus save all men and women forevermore.

Nowhere else in the Bible does it say that Adam's transgression condemned all mankind. Nowhere. It is part of the mythology that Paul comes up with for his new religion knowing that the Gentiles would not know any better. Paul's version of the burgeoning new religion labeled Christianity was cult-like in its self-serving message of free forgiveness through grace and its dependence on its leaders for telling people how they should act absent the law. Paul's letters contain a laundry list of do's and don'ts. (See Appendix) Paul's rules are a natural consequence when you have any group of people acting on what a non-existent holy Spirit is telling them. The default spirit becomes their own egos and they do what they want thinking they are good people because they have the holy Spirit working in them. The process is absolutely no different from that of the Israelites who were unable to follow the Ten Commandments. They defaulted to doing what they wanted. Aaron and Moses stepped in with Mosaic law to control a population of people who were going this way and that doing what they wanted and harming themselves and the community in the process. That is what all laws and rules do. They control the behavior of people who cannot control themselves. Once we submit ourselves to these laws, then we tangentially submit ourselves to the people in control of implementing these rules and laws.

The members of Paul's churches submitted themselves to all the rules and regulations Paul's own ego came up with and Christian churches have been following his example ever since. Unfortunately, Paul's ego had a strong aversion to both women and homosexuals and those two groups of people have paid a heavy price ever since, depending upon how strongly the churches have adhered to Paul's brand of Christianity versus the teachings of the actual man Jesus. Unfortunately, the default has been Paul's brand of Christianity because many of Jesus' teachings have been lost or purposely destroyed by the leaders of the church who hold their positions due to the original structure created by Paul. Why would they want to give up those positions by exposing and teaching the true message of Jesus when the true message of Jesus would topple the structure because of the responsibility it places on each and every individual human being to work at their own soul's salvation through the process of self-examination, repentance and forgiveness.

The laws of consciousness that Jesus and the prophets said will save us because they protect the individual as well as the community became the ministry of death in Paul's view. Paul turned the law and the prophets on its ear. He turned the entire Bible upside down with his 'New Covenant' and Christian leaders are having a hell of a time trying to get it right side up because of all the confusion Paul threw into the mix.

The modern-day church could provide a very valuable service that would be in great demand if it were to get away from Paul and begin disseminating the consciousness teachings of Jesus that focus on the improvement of the individual mind. The church has what I believe is the solution for creating peace on the planet by applying Jesus' methods for creating peace within the individual mind. It does not need to resort to manipulations when the truth would have people returning to the church in droves. First, however, it must reject the doctrine of Paul and reconnect to the Old Testament teachings on consciousness that were begun by Moses and came to fruition through Jesus.

Paul's Manipulation of the Truth

Paul completely destroyed what Moses created on Mt. Sinai, but he sure did love using Moses as his example. In one instance, Paul is defending himself before the church at Corinth when its members begin to question the validity of his teachings after hearing a different gospel from people Paul disparagingly refers to as false apostles, deceitful workers, who masquerade as apostles of Christ and superapostles who are in no way superior to him. (2 Corinthians 11:4-5, 11) Using a strategy of manipulation, Paul tries to make the Corinthians questioning him feel guilty for believing what the actual apostles of the living Christ are teaching them. He goes on about how much he has sacrificed to preach to them for free, asking them, "Did I make a mistake when I humbled myself so that you might be exalted, because I preached the gospel of God to you without charge? *I plundered other churches by accepting from them in order to minister to you.*" (2 Corinthians 11:7-8)

In his efforts to sidestep their concerns with arguments about how much he has sacrificed for them, Paul gives them what should have been their biggest concern of all. In singing his own praises he slips by telling them he is gouging the churches he is founding with his wide open highway to heaven doctrine. Paul admits he is plundering churches to build more churches. He apparently took money from people who could not afford to give it - if what Paul says the Jerusalem Council warned him about in Galatians 2:9-10 is true - and he used it to build his physical empire of Gentile churches.

Robbing Peter to pay Paul is an age old strategy of justifying theft in the name of the common good of all. It is the Robin Hood strategy for equalizing a playing field that should never be unequal to begin with. If our playing fields are unequal, we should be getting to the root cause for why that is instead of justifying them by taking from one group of people and giving it to another; thereby creating dissension, resentment, bitterness and feelings of unfairness by all the parties involved.

Apparently Paul was on the receiving end of someone's bitterness at his robbing one church to build another. In 1 Corinthians 9:3-9 we find him justifying his actions to those who are passing judgment on him and who does he use as his example? None other than the Moses who he has told the Gentiles to reject:

> "My defense against those who would pass judgment on me is this. Do we not have the right to eat and drink? Do we not have the right to take along a Christian wife, as do the rest of the apostles, and the brothers of the Lord, and Cephas [Peter]? Or is it only myself and Barnabas who do not have the right not to work? Who ever serves as a soldier at his own expense? Who plants a vineyard without eating its produce? Or who shepherds a flock without using some of the milk from the flock? Am I saying this on human authority, or does not the law also speak of these things? It is written in the law of Moses, "You shall not muzzle an ox while it is treading out the grain."

Paul has told all the Gentiles to abandon the law but he pulls it out ever so conveniently when he needs to justify actions for which he is receiving criticism. The law Paul is quoting here was one of the hundreds of laws that Moses and Aaron instituted when the Israelites refused to police themselves by following the ten commandments of consciousness. These hundreds of laws, like our own secular laws, were meant to be taken literally. That is the way you control the behavior of the group when the individuals within the group refuse to control their own behavior. You pass laws. Moses made it a law for the Israelites not to muzzle an ox while it is

treading out the grain for whatever reason he had to make it a law –
probably to let the ox freely eat grain while it is working. Paul, the
master of the metaphysical interpretation when it serves his
purposes, turns this very literal law into a justification for him to
reap a monetary harvest from his churches.

In his own words, Paul was educated at the feet of Gamaliel
strictly in the ancestral laws. He knew the true intent of this law.
The same cannot be said of the members of his church at Corinth.
Paul could say whatever he wanted concerning scriptures and they
would have been none the wiser because they did not have the same
level of education he had. He knew this very well. Paul knew well it
was not God speaking here; that it was Moses the lawgiver. Yet the
literal interpretation this verse was meant to convey did not serve to
provide the metaphor Paul needed to justify his reaping a harvest of
material wealth off the seed of the Corinthians' money. His
argument must have worked exceedingly well because it is still being
used to this day to convince the people filling church pews each
Sunday morning to fill the offering plate with their generous
donations. The plates get filled because many of people filling
church pews today rely on their pastors and priests for their
information as much as the Corinthians relied on Paul because they
hate reading the Bible for themselves and coming to their own
conclusions about what it says.

The Question of Circumcision

Paul would have continued reaping an abundant harvest from his
churches if he had not begun running into problems with Jews who
were telling the uncircumcised Gentiles that they cannot be saved
unless they are circumcised in accordance with Mosaic practice.

Although "there arose no little dissension and debate by Paul and Barnabas with them, it was decided that Paul, Barnabas and some of the others should go up to Jerusalem to talk to the apostles and presbyters about this question." (Acts 15:2)

I would say that *no little dissension and debate* is an understatement. Paul does some of his best metaphysical somersaults trying to justify why the uncircumcised Gentiles should not be required to have themselves circumcised. In order to give the Gentiles a get-out-of-jail-free card with regard to this very physical procedure, he comes up with a rationalization to beat all rationalizations by telling them, "Circumcision, to be sure, has value if you observe the law; but if you break the law, your circumcision has become uncircumcision. Again, if an uncircumcised man keeps the precepts of the law, will he not be considered circumcised?" (Romans 2:25-26)

What Paul is arguing here is that the Gentiles can disregard this one eensy, teensy law if they comply with all the others because, after all, they are already not in compliance with this law. It is like grandfathering in a law. It is also like Paul's beliefs on the forgiveness of sins where our sins don't count because all past, present and future ones are covered by the blood of Jesus. Paul makes it up as he goes. It is what all lawmakers and politicians do when they create laws favorable to one group of people but exclude others. It is pandering at its worst.

Paul continues his tortuous rationalizations of why Gentiles do not have to be circumcised by saying, "One is not a Jew outwardly. True circumcision is not outward, in the flesh. Rather, one is a Jew inwardly, and circumcision is of the heart, in the spirit, not the letter; his praise is not from human beings but from God." (Romans 2:28) Paul is trying to convince his audience that the physical act of circumcision is not a physical act after all. It is actually a state of mind. Circumcise your thoughts of evil from your heart and you are good to go. Paul did this all the time. He used metaphysical interpretations for the specific statutory laws of Moses. It would be like me arguing that speeding is not actually speeding at all. It is merely a way for me to expedite my growth in knowing God. It is ridiculous and Paul knew it was ridiculous, but he had to redefine the laws, particularly this law, because adult Gentiles were not about to have themselves circumcised in order to receive salvation. His churches would be empty.

The Council of Jerusalem

The Jews were upset that the laws were being relaxed for the Gentile Christians and the Gentiles were upset that they had to follow a bunch of laws to become converts. This split came to such a boiling point, particularly with regard to circumcision, that Paul and Barnabus felt it necessary to go to Jerusalem at the end of their first mission trip to get feedback from the apostles and presbyters about this question. (Acts 15:2) Paul is welcomed by the apostles and church presbyters when he enters Jerusalem for the council meeting but there are "some from the party of the Pharisees who had become believers who stood up and said, 'It is necessary to circumcise them and direct them to observe the Mosaic law.'" (Acts 15:5) The apostles and presbyters decide to meet with Paul in a closed door meeting outside the presence of these Pharisees to decide the matter.

No doubt Paul relayed to them during this meeting the incident involving Barnabas and him in Iconium where their holy Spirit gospel gained them a great number of both Jewish and Greek followers who heard them preach it in the synagogue. Their great success, however, caused many of the disbelieving Jews to stir up and poison the minds of the Gentiles against them. (Acts 14:1-2) It is quite likely that many of these same Jews were the among the Pharisees protesting outside the Council of Jerusalem. What is clear from the passages in Acts and Romans is that the split between Jew and Gentile never involved the question of whether or not Jesus was the Messiah. It arose out of bitterness and resentment on the part of some Jews who thought it unfair that their salvation required them to follow all the burdensome laws of Moses, while the Gentiles were getting salvation for free. Jesus and his teachings are made a moot point by the time Paul appears on the scene and changes the message completely. Like all propaganda adopted as truth, the real truth got buried under false assumptions accepted as fact. It is a legitimate question to debate what kind of Messiah the Jews were expecting and whether or not Jesus fit the bill, but that is a question that was left unanswered and continues to be left unanswered because the Christians created by Paul have not been given the teachings that Jesus gave about the role of an individual consciousness in determining good and evil. Those teachings were labeled as heresy by the Council of Nicaea and the apostolic gospels and letters that focused on them were banned.

The Messiah who forgives sin through his death and resurrection is a myth that Paul claims to have received from the spirit of Jesus in his visions. Actually, myth is not the right word for it. Propaganda may be a more appropriate description of Paul's visionary proclamations. The Miriam Webster Dictionary defines propaganda as "ideas or statements that are often false or exaggerated and that are spread in order to help a cause, a political leader, a government, etc." Paul's false ideas he claimed to have received from the spirit of Jesus were used for the cause of building a religion to support a hierarchy of leaders that Paul personally appointed to each church. (Acts 14:21-27) He interpreted Old Testament scriptures to conform to the world view he was selling that Jesus delivers the holy Spirit to us from God through his intermediaries in the church. That is what propaganda does. It uses word plays to extract meanings from credible sources that fit the story we want told.

Paul was not the only disciple with a penchant for propaganda though. During the closed door meeting Paul and Barnabas have with Peter, James and John at the Council of Jerusalem, they all consciously decide to twist the words of the prophets to come up with a story and strategy that will make it easy for Paul and Barnabas to continue attracting Gentiles to their churches, while at the same time trying to appease the Jews who want the Gentiles to follow the same laws they are required to follow. Almost immediately, their self-righteous talk turns to what they can do to get both the Jews and Gentiles to shut up about their concerns while their work of empire building continues unabated. There was absolutely no talk in this meeting about resolving the resistance they were receiving from the Jews who were protesting outside the meeting, but not allowed into the meeting. There was no attempt to get to the root cause of their concerns so that they could be properly addressed and changes made. There was no turning to what Jesus may have thought about the matter even though they named their theology after Jesus and used him as their shield of honor and integrity. No. Their goal was to continue building churches. Their focus immediately became how they could get around the law of circumcision to continue attracting Gentiles while appeasing the Jews who were angered at the inherent unfairness of exempting Gentiles from circumcision if salvation for everyone is the goal of all from a theological standpoint.

Nothing holy, sacred or even truthful took place in that Council meeting which is described in Acts, Chapter 15. It was a political meeting used to carve out a political strategy of following the path of least resistance. Political strategists could learn a great deal from studying what happened at that Council meeting. Perhaps they already have. Maybe we should consider the possibility that the Bible has been deemed irrelevant and outdated so that we do not acquire the same level of knowledge they have with regard to the evil of the political process and the people we let control us with self-interested agendas that are compiled in closed door meetings like the one these "holy" men held at the Council of Jerusalem. It is a sickening display when viewed from the perspective of the Gentiles and Jews who these men claimed to serve. The Gentiles and Jews were considered by these leaders of the church as nothing more than pieces on a gameboard to be moved around and manipulated to win their game of empire building. Not one word was uttered about the human soul. Not one word was uttered about how the salvation they were supposedly providing to their followers was completely eradicated with their propaganda. Nothing was mentioned about Jesus and how he may have viewed the matter.

We have remained so blind for so long about how so many

people at the top of our political, educational, religious, business and cultural pyramids come up with strategies of manipulation and deceit in their closed door meetings in order to hand them out to their respective disciples in the hierarchical row below to spread out to the mass of people in the bottom rows. Although they use propaganda to convince the people below that these agendas are to their benefit, the truth says otherwise. They create them in secret behind closed doors so that the truth never becomes known. These agendas are nothing other than strategies of self interest to keep themselves in power so that they control the message to reap the maximum amount of benefit to themselves. That is how egoistic power players think the game gets won - in secret manipulations of the truth not open to discussion by outsiders.

The closed door meeting at the Council of Jerusalem was a hotbed of manipulations, justifications and lies; so much so that it makes one wonder if the men in attendance were not trying just as hard to convince themselves that what they were planning to do was honorable. "After much debate," Acts 15:6-12 tells us, "Peter got up to speak." He tells the assembly that as the one chosen by God to give the message of the Gospel to the Gentiles, he sees no benefit in placing any extra burden on them over and above what the holy Spirit requires of them. Barnabas and Paul then get up and describe all the "signs and wonders God has worked among the Gentiles through them." As if Peter's proclamation and the testimony of Paul and Barnabas is not enough, James also gets up and agrees with the positions they have taken. In support of their united front, James quotes a passage in the Old Testament Book of Amos that foresees a day coming when "the one who plows shall overtake the one who reaps and the vintager, the sower of the seed. The mountains shall drip with the juice of grapes, and all the hills shall run with it." (Amos 9:13)

What Amos is saying when he says the one who plows (the worker) shall overtake the one who reaps (the one making a profit off the work of the one who plows) is that we will eventually evolve to the place where humanity does not have a hierarchical system of dividing equal human beings into rows of power and perceived value. At that stage of our evolution, we will all eat and drink what we all plant and grow:

> Amos 9:11: "On that day I [God] will raise up the fallen hut of David; I [God] will wall up its breaches, raise up its ruins, and rebuild it as in the days of old … I will restore my people Israel, they shall rebuild and inhabit their ruined cities, Plant vineyards and drink the wine, set out gardens and eat the fruits. I will plant them upon their own ground; never again shall they be plucked from the land I have given them. The LORD, your God, has spoken."

According to Amos, Israel is not a physical land that God inhabits. It is the natural human state of mind where the truth resides. This earth was created for the use of all men and women. We are all meant to eat and drink the fruits of the land given to us as our birthright. People were never meant to be plucked and singled out for purposes of control and to be controlled, which is what hierarchical systems do. There are no favored nations and no favored people. There are only God's people of which we are all one. Amos is saying that one day our minds will be aligned with truth and the paradigm will shift from the master/slave, ruler/ruled mentality of our present pyramidal system of command and control to the consciousness framework of Moses who saw the benefit of all people following the same set of rules to rebuild and inhabit an earth that sustains and prospers us all equally:

> Amos 9:7-9: "Did I not bring the Israelites from the land of Egypt as I brought the Philistines from Caphtor and the Arameans from Kir? See, the eyes of the Lord GOD are on this sinful kingdom, and I will destroy it from the face of the earth."

The sinful kingdom referred to in the above passage is the one that rests in corrupted minds like Caiaphas who feel it is their right to kill the messengers of truth because they fear what the truth will do to the positions and ill-gotten power they have received through a system of hierarchy. When a glass of polluted water is turned upside down, the scum rises to the top. Likewise, the mental scum of a corrupted mind can more often than not be an asset in a topsy-turvy, pyramidal organizational structure where the masses of people suffer at the bottom of a system rigged by the few at the top.

Just as the Bible does not define Israel as a piece of land, God is not going to physically destroy any kingdoms or nations from the face of the earth. Our own consciousness made in the image of the Creator will destroy the ego consciousness whose scum of irrationality, falsehood, propaganda and lies has caused so much human damage and suffering during its time on this earth.

In the hands of a pragmatist like James, the true meaning of the passage in Amos becomes problematic. James was not as interested in spreading the idea of equality and truth as much as he was in creating his own hierarchy of power where he and his fellow travelers in cronyism could control the message. Like Paul, James felt it was within his purview to rewrite problematic scriptures to fit the agenda at hand. The agenda in this particular instance is to build a church of followers from a population that is resistant to adopting the same laws the Jews have to follow. In pursuit of that agenda, James misquotes the passage from Amos to make it more user friendly by quoting it as follows:

> Acts 15:16-18: "After this I shall return and rebuild the fallen hut of David; from its ruins I shall rebuild it and raise it up again, so that the rest of humanity may seek out the Lord, even all the Gentiles on whom my name is invoked. Thus says the Lord who accomplishes these things, known from of old."

In James' hands, God is not our human capacity to act godlike in creating a world where all people are sustained through its shared resources. James makes God an external entity that must be sought out and that is the job of the churches … to lead people to this god in the sky who is separate and apart from its creation. The best way for the church to do that, in the view of Paul, James, Peter and John is by not placing any undue burdens on potential members which may scare them away. (Acts 15:19)

This was a flagrant misuse of language to justify the pandering that these men concluded was required if they were to succeed in their goal of converting Gentiles throughout Asia and the world. James concludes the meeting by saying, "It is my judgment, therefore, that we ought to stop troubling the Gentiles who turn to God, but tell them by letter to avoid pollution from idols, unlawful marriage, the meat of strangled animals, and blood."

The apostles and presbyters, in conjunction with the other

leaders of the church in attendance, decide to write a letter to this effect and send out representatives to deliver it to the Gentiles. The letter reads as follows:

> Acts 15:23-29: "The apostles and the presbyters, your brothers, to the brothers in Antioch, Syria, and Cilicia of Gentile origin: greetings. Since we have heard that some of our number [who went out] without any mandate from us have upset you with their teachings and disturbed your peace of mind, we have with one accord decided to choose representatives and to send them to you along with our beloved Barnabas and Paul, who have dedicated their lives to the name of our Lord Jesus Christ. So we are sending Judas and Silas who will also convey this same message by word of mouth: 'It is the decision of the holy Spirit and of us not to place on you any burden beyond these necessities, namely, to abstain from meat sacrificed to idols, from blood, from meats of strangled animals, and from unlawful marriage. If you keep free of these, you will be doing what is right. Farewell.'"

What James and Peter are saying here is why bother these poor folks with a bunch of rules and regulations which no one can follow anyway? Let's pick a few of the easier ones and tell the Gentiles that if they follow these few, they're good to go. Unbeknownst to the Gentiles who thought they were getting a break from the burdensome laws the Jews had to follow, they merely opened themselves up to all the dos and don'ts that Paul eventually imposes on them to fill the vacuum for a people who have not been given the truth of the law and the prophets. (See Appendix)

The letter was met with delight from the members of the church at Antioch. We always love to have the easy road blessed by those with authority over us and we repay them with our blind loyalty. After an argument with Barnabas, however, Paul parts ways with him and teams up with Silas. Together they travel from city to city delivering the letter from the apostles and presbyters and "day after day, the churches grew stronger in faith and increased in number." (Acts15:36-41, Acts 16:1-5)

5
Sins Of The Flesh

The Devil Makes Paul Do It

Although we know very little about Paul other than what is contained in his letters, he appears to be a man with a lot of internal conflict. Whether it is due to his conversion and guilt over his past actions or whether it is due to his inability to change certain aspects of himself is hard to say. What we can surmise from his letters is that this inner conflict helped create his philosophy of "sins of the flesh."

Before Saul/Paul's conversion, he was a hunter hunting the followers of Jesus who were giving a message similar to the one Stephen gave which got him killed. This message emphasized the Ten Commandments of God that Jesus encapsulated into his two greatest commandments in Matthew 22:37-40 where he said, "Have love for the Lord your God with all your heart, and with all your soul, and with all your mind. This is the first and greatest rule. And a second like it is this, Have love for your neighbour as for yourself. On these two rules all the law and the prophets are based."

When Paul killed Stephen and was going from house to house

dragging men and women out and imprisoning them, he was living outside the law of the commandments and prophets that his conversion would have required him to follow. After his conversion, the pain of the sins he committed in his ignorance would have come to the forefront of his mind, as they do to all people who are willing to look at themselves and situations truthfully and confront the mistakes they have made. Paul would have had to deal with all the shame, regret and guilt of abusing, harassing, arresting, imprisoning and killing innocent people while he was acting under the direction of the Sanhedrin and their laws regarding blasphemy.

It was not the Gentiles Paul was killing. It was his fellow Jews. If Paul was not a Pharisee plant used for purposes of misdirection by changing the message of Jesus, then he truly may have been feeling guilt over killing his fellow Jews. However, he would have been in a difficult position. It appears that he was probably a member of the Sanhedrin when he killed Stephen and other followers of Jesus. He would have put his Pharisee buddies in a very bad way if he apologized for the crimes of the state in such a public manner. An apology would have put him in the crosshairs of a Jewish leadership who would have destroyed him for his perceived betrayal of them and it could have started a domino effect within the general Jewish population to take action against a corrupt leadership that was using them for its own end. One never goes against a corrupt gang without suffering the consequences.

After his conversion, Paul would have realized that the only crime his victims committed was to follow the commandments of God, which Paul himself was then wanting to follow as a convert. He killed and imprisoned the very people among whom he wanted to be counted after his conversion. How does one do that after having caused so much suffering and heartache for people who are now your colleagues? How does a person deal with the guilt of horrible acts committed against one's own fellow men and women while ignorant of the truth? How could Paul ever find peace of mind knowing that the acts he committed in ignorance that caused so much pain and loss could never be taken back? They could never be undone.

I am certain these are questions that Paul asked himself every waking minute because I feel his pain when I read what he writes in Romans 7:9-11:

> "I once lived outside the law, but when the commandment came, sin became alive; then I died, and the commandment that was for life turned out to be death for me. For sin, seizing an opportunity in the commandment, deceived me and through it put me to death."

I, the woman who began her study of Paul hating the man, can almost cry for him when I read where he says that the commandment that was for life became death for him. He was in torment when he wrote those verses. Paul is describing here the anguish that always comes when we decide to be truthful with ourselves. The process of self-examination always brings pain. True conversions are very painful. These verses make me sad because Paul was on the precipice of enlightenment, and he turned back. This was the point in his life where he could have attained to the Christ-like consciousness that Jesus achieved in his own wilderness journey; but instead of entering into the pain, analyzing it and feeling it so that he could feel it in other people, Paul doubled down on his efforts to bury the pain by abandoning the laws of consciousness that were bringing it to the forefront of his mind and making him feel like he wanted to die.

The emotions generated by a mind that is no longer ignorant of reality can become overwhelming because the sins committed in ignorance come into full view and must be addressed. That is what penance is. It is the process of coming to know ourselves for the first time freed of the labels society has given us to define ourselves. When a person is unable to deal with mistakes, regret and past choices that resulted in so much harm to others by dealing with them truthfully, that energy has to go somewhere. In Paul's case, it manifested as self-hatred which he openly talks about when he tells his church:

> "What I do, I do not understand For I do not do
> what I want but I do what I hate. Now if I do what I
> do not want, I concur that the law is good, So now it
> is no longer I who do it, but sin that dwells in me. For
> I know that good does not dwell in me, that is, in my
> flesh." (Romans 7:15)

Paul freely admits he hates what it is he is doing. He is aware that whatever it is he did or continues doing is wrong, but he does not have a will strong enough to examine and change the internal thoughts and emotions that are driving the behavior. Instead, he abdicates responsibility for his doing by separating his actions (the flesh that does what he does not want it to do) from his mind (the holy Spirit of Jesus that lives in his mind). Paul explains this dichotomy of flesh and spirit as follows:

"But, if I do that which I have no mind to do, I am in agreement with the law that the law is good. So it is no longer I who do it, but the sin living in me. For I am conscious that in me, that is, in my flesh, there is nothing good: I have the mind but not the power to do what is right. For the good which I have a mind to do, I do not: but the evil which I have no mind to do, that I do. But if I do what I have no mind to do, it is no longer I who do it, but the sin living in me. So I see a law that, though I have a mind to do good, evil is present in me." (Romans 7:16-21)

To Paul, sin is a force within his body over which he has no control. Paul refers to this force as the devil. (Ephesians 4:26, Ephesians 6:11, 1 Timothy 3:6-7, 2 Timothy 2:25-26) Thus, Paul reasons, if he does something wrong, it is the devil making him do it - not Paul himself. If it is a force outside himself making him do what he hates, then he cannot be blamed because although he controls his "spirit" self, the devil is in control of his bodily members:

"So, then, I discover the principle that when I want to do right, evil is at hand. For I take delight in the law of God in my inner self, but I see in my members another principle at war with the law of my mind. taking me captive to the law of sin that dwells in my members. Miserable one that I am! Who will deliver me from this mortal body? Thanks be to God through Jesus Christ our Lord. Therefore, I myself with my mind, serve the law of God but, with my flesh, the law of sin." (Romans 7:21-25)

When I read this verse, it is as if I feel a light bulb going off in Paul's head. He is trying so hard to find an excuse for what he is doing so that he does not have to feel so bad about it. He tells himself that he is thinking all the right things (as he heard Jesus tell his followers) but he is still doing what is wrong. He ponders this dilemma for awhile, and then comes his eureka moment … that's it. It is not the holy Spirit that dwells in my mind causing me to sin. It is the devil that dwells within my physical body. Whew. What a relief. Thanks be to Jesus that I am able to serve the law of God within my mind while still committing sin within my limbs.

Talk about having your cake and eating it too. Paul was the poster child for psychopaths, narcissists and other egocentric personality types who are completely unable to take responsibility for their actions. This is a total abdication of personal responsibility through the use of fairy tales. It is like a child telling a parent that the monster under the bed made the mess in the room, not him. It is also a fairy tale that places the focus on the *do* of our behavior because it focuses on the physical body as the catalyst for our morality. If what we do is good, then we are good. If what we do is bad, then we are bad. Paul couldn't have that though, so he created a holy Spirit of good that lives in his mind and has sovereignty over his physical body. It has the power to forgive him all his transgressions past, present and future. Forgiveness is always at hand in Paul's world because Jesus died for our fleshly sins and lives in our minds if we make a simple request to "have him come into our lives." The church was only institutionalizing Paul's reasoning when it created the confessional. How convenient and how ghastly that this weak, egoistic and manipulative man's schizophrenic doctrine was made official church doctrine and the man himself was canonized.

There is no room in Paul's words to give this belief system a metaphysical meaning as so many religious leaders try to do when they say that fleshly sins are wrong thoughts and negative emotions. In so doing, they always quote Paul's renewal of the mind verse in Romans 12:2 that reads as follows:

> "And do not be conformed to this world, but be transformed by the renewing of your mind, so that you may prove what the will of God is, that which is good and acceptable and perfect." (Romans 12:2)

Paul is telling us in this verse to renew our minds so that we think on good things because that is the domain of the holy Spirit which we must keep pure. Our mind, in Paul's view, is a sacred domain that must be kept pure while our flesh is wicked and full of sin. Paul told his followers to renew their minds and then he immediately gave them a litany of rules they should follow because he soon found out that people have a difficult time discerning what is coming from the holy Spirit and what is coming from their own egos when they have no standards by which to judge their behavior. Our ego consciousness can rationalize any action we take into being something good in our own minds. Only a mind grounded in the commandments of consciousness knows that what is harmful to its own consciousness is likewise harmful to the consciousness of a fellow human being. For instance, we do not like to be stolen from, therefore we should not steal. We do not like to be lied to, therefore we should not lie. We would not like our spouse to cheat on us, therefore we should not cheat on our spouse. This is the logic inherent in Jesus' command to do unto others as you would have done to you, but only a mind that recognizes the commonality of life inherent in all human life would see the benefit of following that command.

It is the same with stealing, murder, rape, gossip, and all the other forms of behavior that one may commit without first considering how that external behavior may affect one's own mind and the minds of others when one seeks to live in reality. You simply cannot separate the behavior from the mind (or the yeast from the dough) because one affects the other. Priests who molest young children would understand this if they were following the teachings of Jesus and not the theology of Paul. Flesh and mind are one and the same.

Paul's separation of mind from the flesh is the foundation of his doctrine of grace. The holy Spirit is always available to forgive us our sins of the flesh when we renew our minds. Grace, under Paul's definition, creates what in computer programming would be called an infinite loop. An infinite loop occurs in a computer program when the coding lacks a functional exit so that the program just keeps repeating the same instruction over and over and over again with no end — similar to a hamster riding its wheel. In Paul's doctrine of grace, forgiveness is always at hand. It requires nothing from us in terms of learning, growth or change. It is a stagnant doctrine that keeps its followers from a forward progress that self-examinatioh would provide them because it allows them to continue doing what they are doing believing that forgiveness is always at hand as long as they renew their minds with good thoughts.

Paul was unable to deal with his own shame and guilt in a truthful manner and he built his belief system around this avoidance. To this day, pastors continue to view guilt and shame as sinful rather than the natural result of a mind that realizes its sins. By making these emotions the sinful part of the equation, rather than the acts that elicited these emotions, Paul and these pastors deny their followers the very salvation they claim to be providing.

Although the common belief is that Adam and Eve felt ashamed after eating the fruit from the tree of knowledge of good and evil, the fact of the matter is that the Bible never says they felt ashamed after eating the fruit. It was, in fact, their failure to feel any shame or guilt that prevented them from ever admitting their wrongdoing when truth came calling in the form of God.

Shame, regret and guilt are not the bad emotions the pastors promoting grace and secularists promoting positive thinking would have a person believe. They are the path to salvation. They are the inevitable result of realizing the mistakes we made in ignorance of the truth. By telling people that grace forgives them for everything they have ever done and that there is no place for guilt and shame, the feelings never get dealt with and the sincere and true apologies that should be provided to the victims of acts done in our ignorance are never given. There is all this excess negative energy that never gets balanced out. It has to go somewhere and so it goes inward. People become too ashamed of themselves to apologize while their victims wait for an apology that never comes.

Protection of one's self image is an extremely powerful force. That is why the non-apology apology is so popular. It gives the appearance of repentance without suffering the consequences. When Paul attributes his killings and imprisonments as acts done under the law, that is exactly what he is doing. He is acknowledging his wrong acts but he justifying them as legal. He is essentially saying, 'sorry, not sorry.' By using the law to justify his breaking of one of the commandments that became death to him, Paul condemned himself not only to a life of inner turmoil, but also to one in which he would repeat the same mistakes he made in his previous career working at the behest of the chief priests.

Paul condemned himself to the same dust of the ground that Adam and Eve do when they are unable to face the truth and admit what they did was wrong. (Genesis 3:14-24) Evil is self-hatred that manifests in malevolent actions and like Paul, most people have buried the causes of their self-hatred deep within their psyches. Narcissists like Paul have the ability to bury them extremely deep so that they can continue doing what they do. They are the most unaware people on the planet and therefore the most dangerous because they have lost all connection to their source of life. Consequently, they have lost the connection to the life source of their fellow men and women.

In the following chapter, I discuss how Paul became a prolific user of some of the patterns of evil I identify in my book, *Morality Within the Framework of Reality*. They were strategies that brought him success in his previous career as a Pharisee enforcer, so he uses them in his new career as the builder of Gentile churches. If he had done the self-examination he needed to do, he would have realized these strategies are the creation of deluded minds like Eve's which want to avoid truth by sneaking around it in order to get what they personally want. In Eve's case, what she wanted was the forbidden fruit. In Paul's case, it was the recognition, power and prestige that would come to him by building a religious empire under his personal control. He retained his own ego consciousness and created his own delusions to sneak around the true message of Jesus in order to achieve that goal.

My Letter to Paul of Tarsus

During my darkest moments of depression and dissociation after a workplace mobbing forged against me, I remember desperately thinking to myself, 'I want to go home;' having no earthly idea where home was or why I was thinking it so strongly and clearly within a brain that was so foggy, lost and consumed with untangling the prior events that took place at my workplace which were making no sense to me at all.

It has been over 15 years since the mobbing and in that time, I have come home to the place for which my mind was longing all those many years ago; although it has taken many twists and turns in my thought process to find the home that my dissociated mind instinctively knew existed.

What I know now is that my mind was my inborn protector and guide while my brain was completely dysfunctional and unfocused. The two are not the same and by merging them into one, as I did and the secular community at large has done, we have given up a vital tool in our human makeup that protects and guides us in navigating this physical world.

Talking of God turns many people off because we have turned 'him' into an intangible being that lives in the sky that only becomes tangible to one who adopts a religion. And in the beginning of my journey home, it was the pastor at a Christian church who gave me great comfort every Sunday with his wonderful sermons on love and forgiveness. I will be forever grateful to him for that because it lit a small light in my brain that I believe gave me the strength to continue on in my quest for the knowledge my mind instinctively knew I needed if I was ever to find an escape from the dissociative state I was in.

The first major step was learning the value of truth and confronting the company and all the mobbing participants with the truth in an email I sent to them a year and a half later. Almost immediately, the strange occurrences that were happening in my life and leading me towards a psychotic breakdown stopped. In their tracks. I now know for certain there was some gang stalking going on, though I may never know whether it was the company doing it or particular individuals within the company responsible for it. Gang stalking is a terrifying but very real thing. So for everyone who is currently experiencing it I would say, don't doubt yourself and think you are crazy. You were not feeling crazy until those odd occurrences started happening, right? Therefore, when you hear something like a conversation on a bus or in a bookstore where people are recounting exactly what happened to you as if it happened to them, don't run away. Muster the courage to join the conversation and watch how quickly the stalkers disperse. If you think you are being followed, you probably are. In that case, tell yourself, 'so what' and continue on. Do not confront them because they will make you look like the crazy one. It is depraved and/or desperate/greedy people who become gang stalkers. Always do what protects you and your own mind. If you follow truth and do what is right in all circumstances, your own mind will protect and guide you, even though you may not always be aware of it. It is the conscious and subconscious part of you that is always running in the background, collating emotions, thoughts, information and experiences that could be centuries old given what I am about to tell you,

Many scientists and physicists now think the universe itself is a conscious mind of sorts. I say, of course it is. Philosophers as old as Pythagoras and religious teachers as old Jesus believe what modern proponents of the big bang theory believe. And that is that the universe explosively grew from one small seed (see Jesus's parable of the mustard seed), or one divine number (see the Pythagorean prayer) or a single particle that exploded and expanded to become the universe (see the big bang theory).

If these theories are correct, then the tiny seed, number or particle is what we human beings have been calling God. Is the seed still contained within the mustard tree? No. The seed is the mustard tree. The divine number is the eternally flowing creation and the particle is the universe that is forever growing and expanding. As part of that eternally flowing and expanding universe we are within the seed of creation, and it is within us. I firmly believe it was the seed of creation that kept me moving with a positive and forward-moving momentum when I made the decision I didn't want to remain in a depressed and dissociative state forever. I focused my brain on answering three questions I had after the mobbing and that research led me to the truth of not only the people I viewed as my enemies, but also of myself. What I found is that I had gotten so far away from the seed of creation that is my own mind by immersing myself in this physical world and trying so hard to climb the ladder of success in order to find some sense of fulfillment. When the company gave me my dream job, I became so attached to it that it nearly destroyed me when they took it away. They took away what my brain had made my foundation, and I fell into the abyss until I was able to realize I had a firmer foundation within me that can never be taken away. It is what my own mind was calling home during those very dark days.

And home is where I intend to stay as I eternally grow and expand within the confines of the physical space we call our universe.

6
The Delusion Of Hierarchy

A mind like Paul's views life hierarchically. The lives at the top of the pyramid control the lives of the ones below. Peter, Paul and James viewed their roles at the top of the Church pyramid as the rulers of the converted Christians below. It was their job to direct the lives of the people occupying the rows below. That is why they took it upon themselves to decide which commandments and laws the Gentiles should have to follow and which ones they shouldn't have to follow and used the letter to distribute their revised laws to the churches. They played with the concept of God for the purposes of their own agendas, rather than seeking the God within themselves to create the agenda. That is what authoritarians do. In that way, they make themselves the god leaders who pass out their agendas to the people under their control in the rows below. It is a top-down structure of viewing the world, rather than the horizontal structure that Jesus and the prophets envisioned.

Paul did not want to part with this structure. It is what he knew and it was an environment he was comfortable working within. In Philippians 4:8, Paul says:

> "Finally, brethren, whatsoever things are true, whatsoever things *are* honest, whatsoever things *are* just, whatsoever things *are* pure, whatsoever things *are* lovely, whatsoever things *are* of good report; if *there be* any virtue, and if *there be* any praise, think on these things."

Paul follows up this verse up by telling his audience, "The things you have learned and received and heard and seen in me, practice these things, and the God of peace will be with you." This is Paul's monkey see, monkey do brand of authoritarianism. He encourages his followers to think good things and then use him as a role model for their behavior. All of Paul's dos and don'ts I have attached as an appendix to this book are eerily similar to all the dos and don'ts I was given in the Baptist church of my youth, and which continue to thrive in churches of all denominations to this day. All of Paul's rules regarding hierarchy and women have served to keep women in subordinate positions within the Christian church and within many Christian homes. So many women have suffered because of Paul. Jesus was making women his disciples while Paul was telling them to shut up and ask their husbands how they should think:

> "As in all the churches of the holy ones, women should keep silent in the churches, for they are not allowed to speak, but should be subordinate, as even the law says. But if they want to learn anything, they should ask their husbands at home. For it is improper for a woman to speak in the church." (1 Corinthians 14:33-36)

And in Ephesians 5:22-23 he writes:

"Wives should be subordinate to their husbands as to the Lord. For the husband is head of his wife just as Christ is head of the church."

Many Christian preachers love to preach this false doctrine when they can get away with it. I attended a bible study not too long ago where the most outspoken and confident woman in the group said that her first marriage failed because she did not submit to her husband. When she continued to be the strong personality she naturally was with her second husband, she said her pastor reminded her that it was important she remember to submit to her husband's wishes as he was the head of the household.

Paul was a product of his environment, not a product of Christ's teachings. The disciple that Jesus loved and confided to in a way that got Peter so upset was a woman. It was women who showed up to the crucifixion and it was women who would have anointed Jesus' body while the men were all hiding. The reason Jesus was not a male chauvinist like Paul or Peter was because he read and understood the scriptures with a consciousness that recognizes the inherent equality of all human beings in consciousness – male and female alike.

God is the great equalizer which is why hierarchical systems of rule try to eradicate the concept of God. It is also why when they do that, they eradicate the spark of life that gives us our meaning and reason for being. Our growth as human beings becomes stilted and dies when we are forced to conform to another human being's rules and regulations for how we should live, rather than being given the freedom to explore the world on our own terms within the parameters of a consciousness that recognizes and respects life.

When that pastor told the woman in my Bible study to submit to her husband's authority, he was telling her to turn all her personal feelings and decision-making over to another person who would decide for her. He essentially told her to give up her purpose and meaning in life because that is exactly what we do when we hand our own consciousness over to another person to structure our lives for us. If that person is operating with an ego consciousness like Paul's, it will require us to follow rules that are contrary to our own well-being. Resignation, depression, confusion, stress, anxiety, worry, anger, resentment and bitterness are the natural result.

Paul set the growth of women backwards with his doctrine, while Jesus was exalting the role of women in his ministry. Jesus was teaching Mary how to be confident and self-assured while working among a group of male chauvinist disciples [particularly Peter] who Jesus was trying to teach how to be human. In the Gospel of Thomas there is an exchange between Peter and Jesus where Peter tells Jesus, "Let Mary leave us, as women are not worthy of life." Jesus responds to Peter's unbelievable request and belief by telling him, "I myself will lead her in order to make her male, so that she too may become a living spirit resembling you males. For every woman who makes herself male will enter Heaven's Realm."[11]

Jesus wanted Mary to be strong in her resolve. Every woman who makes herself male will enter Heaven's realm does not mean she will become a bitch. It means she will nurture the part of her consciousness that is denied her in her upbringing where she is taught to be a good little girl. If Jesus had been able to complete his work in making Mary male, she never would have cried when Peter accused her of lying when she told him and the other disciples what

Jesus told her in private regarding the nature of our existence. She would have stood her ground and told him to go to hell.

Paul and Peter thoroughly marginalized Jesus and negated his teachings because the teachings as they stood would have required them to give up societal beliefs that were in opposition to what is true regarding the nature of our human *being*. Our consciousness – the real part of ourselves – is neither male nor female. It is neither better nor worse than anyone else. It is the one. It is the unifying factor that brings us all together under the umbrella of humanity. This obvious fact which is hidden by hierarchy, patriarchy and all the other false societal, organizational and cultural constructs used to divide up humanity into groups of people with varying degrees of value is the foundation Jesus and the prophets said we must start from to raise all of humanity up so that the "one who plows shall overtake the one who reaps and the vintager, the sower of the seed. The mountains shall drip with the juice of grapes, and all the hills shall run with it." (Amos 9:13)

The false constructs used for building turfs in the competitive ego-conscious paradigm serve as nothing more than a dangerous game in a fully evolved human consciousness. We must destroy these false constructs of mind if we ever hope to realize our collective humanity. This earth is humanity's birthright, and it has been stolen by people like Peter, James and Paul who use the environmental structures in place to mark their territories. The paradigm of our minds must shift from that of a Paul to that of a Jesus if we are ever to achieve equality for all human beings organically and without harm to the consciousness of any individual or group.

7
Paul's Bullying Tactics

Paul is a Prolific User of the Bully-Bystander-Enabler-Target Model of Behavior

I disliked Paul when I discovered who he actually was without the veil of sainthood. However, I have since concluded that he was only doing what he knew and he was backed up by some of the very apostles who were mentored by Jesus. They thought they were doing good by converting the Gentiles and they were doing it with methods they learned from their leaders that they knew would work. They should serve as an example to us all of how our intentions can be good but our methods wrong.

We all have reasons for thinking the way we do. Indoctrination is forcing a belief system, right or wrong, on someone. If our beliefs are right and true, no indoctrination is required. They spread organically through the population. People are consciousness at their core. We need to let the facts out and speak for themselves. We will eventually come around to a group truth through logic, facts and the training of our individual minds in using logic and facts to come to conclusions. But first, we must begin acting like a race of adults, instead of authoritarian parent leaders and the children they rule. We must take on that responsibility or we will continue to have agendas pushed on us by more powerful people who do not share our beliefs or place the same value on logic and facts in arriving at solutions.

It could be that Jesus was way ahead of his time. Maybe that is why so many Christians await his return. He knew the methods used by the Pharisees because he was as trained in the law as they were. Unlike Paul, when Jesus quoted scripture it was accurate and true. He was debating philosophers, doctors and temple elders at the age of 12. Jesus may have been born a carpenter's son but he advanced through some means to becoming a philosopher who even the Greeks were seeking out. (John 12:20-21) Unlike Paul who used the carrot and stick approach of attracting and keeping followers to his churches, people flocked to hear Jesus. (See Matthew 5:1-2, Matthew 8:1, Matthew 8:18, Matthew 9:35-36, Matthew 14:13-21, Matthew 15:32, Matthew 21:9-11, Mark 2:13, Mark 3:9, Mark 6:34) He did not have to cajole or pressure them into believing what he was saying. They thirsted for it because it was the truth. Paul changed the message and although we may never know with certainty what his motive for doing it was, the results are clear. The treasure trove of knowledge Jesus uncovered and taught his disciples was rejected by the church in favor of Paul's doctrine of dos and don'ts he made up as he went along based on the state of his own egoistic, patriarchal, discriminatory and chauvinistic views. They were the same egoistic, patriarchal, discriminatory and chauvinistic views of early church leaders attending the Council of Nicaea who used bullying tactics to depose, excommunicate, and silence any bishops and ecclesiastics who disagreed with them.[12] The church has been saddled ever since with a doctrine that favors certain people over other people because of the stamp of approval it gave to letters written by a tortured man unable to deal with his character flaws in a truthful manner.

The Bully-Bystander-Enabler-Target Model of Thought and Behavior that I describe in *The Evolution of Good and Evil* is what ego conscious authoritarians rely on to pursue their agendas with as little resistance as possible. The purpose of this model is to frighten, intimidate, pressure, propagandize, slander and punish people into compliance. Through character assassination and stereotyping, the target is placed outside the group/societal norms and thereby becomes an acceptable target for the abuse. For Paul and men like him, women are systemic targets but they are certainly not the only targets. It is where any group can find itself if there is no one outside of the group willing to set these authoritarians in power straight. That is the purpose of the model. To make sure there is no one left to set them straight. The tactics incorporated by the model turn the populations these authoritarians control into bystanders and enablers who are too afraid to take a stand. Paul incorporates almost every single one of these tactics in the creation and maintenance of his Gentile churches. The fact that he incorporates the patterns of evil reinforces my belief that the Gentiles were nothing more than targets for him in filling the pews with their bodies and the offering plates with their money.

Banishment (Cancellation)

In survival environments run by authoritarians, banishment of a member is a very effective form of punishment which ensures that the member who is banished will no longer be able to disrupt the group think mentality of the remaining group members. It guarantees the cohesiveness of the group at the expense of the individual. It is the lazy man's strategy for maintaining order by merely getting rid of the perceived troublemaker. That way, no time or effort has to be expended in trying to resolve any differences through discussion, intervention, reinforcement or any of the other number of conflict resolution techniques available for helping human beings attain the truth and come to amicable solutions among one another. Instead, people who disagree or bring up uncomfortable truths are labeled as troublemakers and are turned into enemies so that the patterns of evil can justifiably be used to punish and silence them without guilt or blame. It is an animal conscious means for resolving conflict which causes so much misery to its human targets.

Paul ran into a situation in the church at Corinth where a man was living with his father's wife. Paul was not present at the church when this scandal arose but that did not stop him from intervening by writing a letter that pronounced judgment on the man in the name of Jesus Christ before even hearing the facts. Paul labeled the man as immoral in his letter and told the church to expel him from its midst and deliver him to Satan "for the destruction of his flesh" so that his spirit can be saved. The passage in 1 Corinthians 5:1-5 reads as follows:

> It is widely reported that there is immorality among you, and immorality of a kind not found even among pagans - a man living with his father's wife. And you are inflated with pride. Should you not rather have been sorrowful? The one who did this deed should be

expelled from your midst. I, for my part, although absent in body but present in spirit, have already, as if present, pronounced judgment on the one who has committed this deed, in the name of [our] Lord Jesus: when you have gathered together and I am with you in spirit with the power of the Lord Jesus, you are to deliver this man to Satan for the destruction of his flesh, so that his spirit may be saved on the day of the Lord.

Notice how Paul does not tell the church it is his judgment that the man is immoral and should be expelled. He tells them he is judging the man in the name of Jesus Christ. He is telling them that Jesus has determined this man is immoral and should be expelled. Claiming he heard from the spirit of Jesus allowed Paul to make these kinds of harsh, life-altering judgments and then hide his vindictiveness behind the name of Jesus. This is beyond the pale in my eyes, but it is what all unaware power brokers do. They will hide behind the names of justice, integrity, honor, freedom and righteousness while passing down judgments that are unjust, vindictive, dishonest and revengeful in nature.

Laws Are Made to Be Rewritten in Paul's World

Paul was an expert in Jewish law and scripture. Tactics provided for in the Bully/Bystander/Enabler/Target Model of Behavior like banishment that are so destructive to the human soul, but justified by the people who use them with righteous reasons, are as old as mankind itself because they are animal conscious tactics we have had centuries of practice at using. The reason they are used is because they work and the people who use them are either completely unaware of the destruction they cause to a human mind or simply do not care.

The Bible's Old Testament is filled with examples of how they are effectively used to destroy perceived enemies. One striking example is found in the Book of Esther. When I first read this story, it was like I was reading a story pulled right out of today's headlines. It felt so modern to me because it is exactly the same "in the interest of national security" strategy our own leaders used and are using to create a massive domestic spy and police agency, take us into endless wars and steal our freedoms from us daily. They opened Pandora's box so that now, even democratic governments are arresting people on charges of terrorism for just speaking their minds.

I have paraphrased the scriptures below but if you would like to read the verses verbatim, they are found in the Book of Esther, Chapters One and Two.

The King's Party

3 In the third year of his rule, King Ahasuerus gave a feast to all his captains and his servants; and the captains of the army of Persia and Media, the great men and the rulers of the divisions of his kingdom were all in attendance;

4 His purpose for the party was to show off the great wealth of his empire.

6 There were exquisite white cotton and royal-blue wool hangings, embroidered with cords of fine linen and purple wool, suspended over silver rods and marble pillars; there were gold and silver couches, on platforms of green, white, shell, and onyx marble.

7 The drinks were served in gold goblets -- no two goblets were alike; royal wine was in abundance, as befits the hand of the king.

8 By ordinance of the king the drinking was unlimited: no one was forced, because the king had instructed his officers to fulfill the wishes of each guest.

The Queen

10 On the seventh day, when the king was under the influence of the wine he had been drinking, he asked his seven eunichs to bring Queen Vashti to him wearing only her royal crown, so that he could show the nations and the ministers her beauty, for she was very beautiful.

Modern Translation:

The king possesses a beautiful object and he wants to show it off. The thought that the queen might feel embarrassed and ashamed of being nude in front of everyone doesn't phase this King. She is an object with no inherent value of her own who answers to him - not the other way around.

12 The Queen refused to come and the king grew angry, and his temper burst.

Modern Translation:

How dare she assert her right as a human being with dignity and value!

The King's Reaction

13 The King spoke to his lawyers, who were familiar with established precedents, because it was the king's custom to confer

with those who knew law and custom.

Modern Translation:

The king is accustomed to consulting with lawyers because they are the experts at getting around the burdensome and difficult to understand laws he and his fellow kings have passed to subjugate the people and keep them in a state of constant confusion over what's allowed and what isn't. He tells them the Queen's refusal is an outrage and that there must be a way to punish the Queen for asserting her right to privacy and personally embarrassing him in the eyes of other nations.

15 The question was: what does the law say should be done to Queen Vashti for not obeying the command that King Ahasuerus conveyed to her through the attendants?

Memuchan's Advice

16 Memuchan said to the king and the ministers, "When Queen Vashti was disobedient, she hurt not only the king but also all the ministers of all the nations in all of the provinces of the king's empire.

Modern Translation:

What a brilliant lie for making it appear that what the Queen did was wrong. It doesn't make any sense or explain how she hurt the king or the ministers by exerting her legal right to privacy and asserting her God-given right not to be shamed and humiliated, but that doesn't really matter. She doesn't matter. They can punish her for bruising the king's ego in front of his colleagues under the guise that her actions not only hurt him, but they also hurt all the other nations within the empire. The old "damaged our national security" argument works every time when we want to limit someone's rights because they threaten our image in some way.

17 When word of the Queen's behavior gets out to all the women, they will treat their husbands with less respect, pointing out that even King Ahasuerus ordered Queen Vashti to come to him and she did not come.

Modern Translation:

If other wives conclude that the Queen was right in doing what she did, then they may try asserting their own rights to privacy and all the husbands who have been using the king's laws to humiliate and shame their wives will risk having their good 'ol boy power network of protecting each other's backs destroyed.

18 This very day, the wives of the ministers of Persia and Media who have heard what Queen Vashti did will bring up this incident to the ministers of the king and that will cause a great deal of scandal and quarreling.

Modern Translation:

We have to find a way to spin this scandal in our favor. We just can't afford to have the plain truth leaking out because that would cause all kinds of problems for us.

19 If it pleases the king, let him issue a royal edict that a new immutable law be written into the laws of Persia and Media to the effect that Queen Vashti may never again come to King Ahasuerus, and that her royal position will be given to someone else more suitable.

Modern Translation:

Even though there are no laws on the books to punish the Queen for doing what she felt was right under the law, we can just adjust the current laws by executive order to make certain the queen is never again able to perform her duties in this realm or any other realm. That'll teach her that no one questions my authority without getting destroyed. We can easily find someone to replace her who will be more than willing to tow the party line and show up nude for all to see whenever I order it.

20 Let the King's decree be posted throughout the entire empire, even though it is very large, and then all the women will respect their husbands, regardless of their status.

Modern Translation:

Let's broadcast this new law on the website, in all our policy guidelines, on the news and in every agency of our kingdom so that all wives will know what happens if they disobey any order from their kings, no matter how humiliating it may be to them personally.

21 The king and the ministers liked this idea, so the king did as Memuchan advised.

Modern Translation:

The group consensus was, "Wow, it doesn't get any better than this. Memuchan is a genius for coming up with this "in the interest of national security" strategy because we can use it over and over again to get what we want and punish people who do not comply with our demands. There is nothing to stop our agenda now. No rules we cannot change and no people we cannot threaten, harass and intimidate into submission.

22 He sent scrolls to all the king's provinces, each scroll written in the alphabet and language of the province to which it was sent, stating that the man is legally the master of his own home, and that everyone in the household must speak the man's native language.

Modern Translation:

Let's make sure everyone, without exception, understands that anyone who tries doing what Queen Vashti did in asserting her human rights will suffer her same fate.

23 The king's personal servants said, "Let them search for beautiful young virgins for the king."

Modern Translation:

No guilt for this king over destroying the Queen's life and putting the kibosh on anyone else who tries doing what she did. His throne is secure because he can always appoint valueless minions and corrupt lawyers willing to do work-arounds of the law for his benefit.

People are not the enemy. Ego is the enemy. In the above passage from Esther, it is one king's ego that destroys the queen's life and then imposes his will on the rest of the people. In organizations like this king's realm, there is no rule of law because he has the power to change the laws to fit any situation he desires. Peter, James and Paul were in the position to change the rules at will. We are told the rule of law protects us, but as the Queen and the Gentiles prove, they all too often protect the power structure.

In *Morality Within the Framework of Reality*, I make the argument that it was Hitler's ego that set in motion all the legal actions that resulted in the Final Solution. It was the ego of Caiaphas that drove him to find a legal forum which would allow for executions when Jesus's influence and message was beginning to threaten his perch on the seat of Jewish power. And it was Peter and Paul's egos that had them easing Jewish laws to attract Gentiles to their churches, rather than building up the character of their individual followers with the messianic message of the man whose legacy they helped destroy by turning him into a god who delivers a non-existent holy Spirit to those who believe in his divinity.

Ego warps everything we think and do because it is the antithesis of reality and truth. Its nature is to self-protect and the most valuable asset we have to protect is our individual images. That is why reputation takes on such importance in our modern world. The more an ego consciousness becomes as asset for success within societal structures, the more valuable reputation becomes over character. When we make it a job qualification for our leaders to be men and women who can "get the job done" when the job that needs to get done is to increase profits for a corporation or protect us from all threats foreign and domestic, then it becomes very easy for these leaders to bend the rules under the justification that they are doing what needs to get done to satisfy the shareholders they are profiting and the citizens they are protecting. Bending the rules does not jive well with a sense of integrity that has a person playing by the rules.

As the leader at the top of the church hierarchy, Paul dictated how its members could create good reputations that would keep them in the good graces of the church and maintain their images as good little Christians. That was the purpose of his orders to the churches that I have called his list of do's and don'ts. I am no longer naive enough to believe that church leaders ever since did not emphasize Paul's orders over Jesus' message for the very same egoistic reasons.

The Pharisee mindset of the Sanhedrin may have silenced Jesus, but it was the mindset of Paul that slandered him by changing his teachings and co-opting his legacy as the Messiah of all people with Paul's bigoted, discriminatory, judgmental and vindictive brand of Christianity. When churches pray "in the name of Jesus" it is code for in the name of whatever leadership is in charge. No one can speak for Jesus except Jesus himself. He spoke and the ones who listened got killed by Paul and they have been getting marginalized, banished and excommunicated ever since by antichrist egos with power. If Jesus were to come back as so many Christians are hoping, how would they ever recognize him if they have been unable to recognize him through the fog of Paul's mythology and lies? The truth was successfully crushed by the antichrist because the antichrist is the antithesis of truth in the name of self.

Ego in all its forms is a usurpation of the reality and truth that defines the God of the universe. It is not even like Paul tries to hide his egoistic God complex. In 1 Corinthians 5:9-13, Paul tells the Corinthians:

> "I wrote you in my letter not to associate with immoral people, not at all referring to the immoral of this world or the greedy and robbers or idolaters; for you would then have to leave the world. But I now write to you not to associate with anyone named a brother, if he is immoral, greedy, an idolater, a slanderer, a drunkard, or a robber, not even to eat with such a person. For why should I be judging

outsiders? Is it not your business to judge those within? God will judge those outside. "Purge the evil person from your midst."

According to Paul, God judges people outside the church but the church itself judges those within its doors and they use the rules that Paul gives them with his long list of dos and don'ts. And this is what churches have been doing for generations. Any pastor who is deemed too liberal in his interpretation of the Bible's scriptures is oftentimes ousted by the more conservative deacons. The deacons have always been the real power players, at least in the Baptist church where I was raised.

Paul was no saint. He was a mean-spirited murderer who brought the murderous mind frame of his Pharisee upbringing into the church. No talk. No trying to understand. No mercy. Just purge the people you do not approve of from your midst.

Threats

When the Corinthians begin asking Paul for proof that he hears directly from the spirit of Jesus, Paul becomes like the parent who does not like having his authority questioned. His tone and manner is like my own father's when I fought with my brothers as a child. If the fighting did not stop after he commanded it to from his recliner in the family room downstairs, he would warn us that he was getting the belt after the count of three. He never had to get the belt because his threat was enough to get us to stop.

In 2 Corinthians 13:1-13, Paul has made two visits to the church at Corinth in response to their requests for evidence that Christ is speaking in him. He is now writing them a letter warning them that if he has to visit for a third time, he will not be lenient in his treatment of them. Paul bases his entire doctrine on what he claims Jesus says to him and yet he acts indignant when his followers ask for some sort of proof that a dead man is talking to him. Then after acting indignant for being questioned about his claims without ever providing them with the evidence they are requesting, he changes the subject entirely by shifting the focus to them:

> "Examine yourselves to see whether you are living in faith. Test yourselves. Do you not realize that Jesus Christ is in you?—unless, of course, you fail the test. I hope you will discover that we have not failed. But we pray to God that you may not do evil, not that we may appear to have passed the test but that you may do what is right, even though we may seem to have failed. For we cannot do anything against the truth, but only for the truth. For we rejoice when we are weak but you are strong. What we pray for is your improvement."

Notice the subtle way in which Paul turns the tables on them by making them think they are weak in their non-belief and need to pray for improvement. This man was a master manipulator. In one sentence he threatens them and in the next cajoles them by telling them their weakness in faith is something they need to work on and he will pray for their improvement. The mind of a manipulator like Paul is the scariest thing on the planet because there is no way to reason with it. It is conscious evil. All you can do is recognize it and try to get away from it.

Paul continues the letter with these words:

> "I am writing this while I am away, so that when I come I may not have to be severe in virtue of the authority that the Lord has given me to build up and

not to tear down."

Talk about using the Lord's name in vain. He knows he's a fraud and he is afraid of being proven for the fraud he is. When a bully is afraid of exposure, he lashes out like a cat in a cage. The Lord has given him authority to build up, in his words, and he will use that authority against them [crush them] if they continue to question him. Like Caiaphas shutting down all talk of Jesus with threats, Paul uses the same technique to shut down any discussion about how he hears from a spirit.

Paul then ends the letter with words of encouragement and love:

> "Finally, brothers, rejoice. Mend your ways, encourage one another, agree with one another, live in peace, and the God of love and peace will be with you. Greet one another with a holy kiss. All the holy ones greet you. The grace of the Lord Jesus Christ and the love of God and the fellowship of the holy Spirit be with all of you."

This is really kind of creepy. Paul has just finished blaming and threatening them and now he is telling them to mend their ways and to love one another. He is a good cop/bad cop all in one. He is the wife beater who abuses his spouse and sends her flowers the next day. This is a masterful, albeit cunningly evil, way of keeping them in line. This behavior is the definition of evil. It is manipulating another person's mind for purposes of controlling it. Cult leaders are masters at this very degenerate form of human behavior control.

Name Calling

The church at Corinth was not the only church expressing doubt about Paul's claims of hearing from the spirit of Jesus. The church at Galatia was also hearing from other teachers whose teachings were in conflict with Paul's. Paul resorts to name calling when questioned by the Galatians:

> Galatians 3:1-3: "Stupid Galatians! Who has bewitched you, before whose eyes Jesus Christ was publicly portrayed as crucified? I want to learn only this from you: did you receive the Spirit from works of the law, or from faith in what you heard? Are you so stupid?"

This doesn't sound like very saintly speech to me. One of the worst sins a person can commit is to call another person stupid. We all have the wisdom of the universe contained within us and if we are stupid, it is because we have refused to conform to the definition of intelligence that Paul and other authoritarians like him always use to make themselves feel superior and more valued on the evolutionary chart. Elitists like Paul always act so surprised when someone without their level of education displays any intelligence. It is the same blindness Caiaphas and the other chief priests had with regard to Peter and the other uneducated apostles. Their natural reaction is to cut the person down by belittling them with tactics like name calling, minimizing their accomplishments, or completely dismissing them. When a person in authority uses this pattern of evil, the destructive effects on a person's mind can last a lifetime because it goes to the core of how the targets of the name calling view themselves. It is bullying at its worst and can never be defended even when the perpetrators are fearful of exposure, as Paul most certainly was.

Isolation To Create a Sense of Shame in The Target

The purpose of the Bully/Bystander/Enabler/Target Model of Thought and Behavior is always to isolate and marginalize the target so that they can be exposed to escalated forms of abuse without any obstacles in the way to stop it. This creates a sense of helplessness and hopelessness in the target of abuse because all avenues for relief are closed to them. They become totally under the control and at the mercy of their abusers. In a universe of infinite possibilities, this targeted state of being is hell. There is no worse state for a human psyche than to be rejected by fellow human beings simply for being who they are and expressing themselves honestly.

Paul loved to use peer pressure to ensure conformance to all his dos and don'ts. In 2 Thessalonians 3:6-7, 14 Paul writes:

> "We instruct you, brothers, in the name of [our] Lord Jesus Christ, to shun any brother who conducts himself in a disorderly way and not according to the tradition they received from us. For you know how one must imitate us. ... <u>If anyone does not obey our word as expressed in this letter, take note of this person not to associate with him, that he may be put to shame.</u>"

Paul was more than willing to create a sense of shame in other people even though he avoided it like the plague in himself. There is a reason why Paul never teaches Jesus' two greatest commandments. They would not have allowed him to use the patterns of evil he used to make his church members conform to his dictates. These two commandments would have required him to treat them as he himself wanted to be treated. As a man who avoided shame at all costs, he would have seen how destructive his policies were to the souls for whom he claimed to have so much love.

Never once does Paul ever refer to these two commandments in his letters. They are central to Jesus' philosophy and they are conspicuously missing from Paul's writings. When a person is unable to honestly examine himself and his motivations, how can he ever know what motivates other people? He cannot. All he has is what he has been taught. These tactics of evil worked for the Pharisee hierarchy in ensuring conformity. When Paul chose to bury his own feelings of guilt and shame after his conversion, he buried his ability to know what these emotions feel like in other people. If he had exposed his mind to the experience, he would never have intentionally engendered those feelings in anyone else – particularly in people who had come to his churches in search of meaning and purpose for their lives. If he had undergone the process of healing his own mind, he would have been able to help the people he was telling his churches to banish, shame and hand over to Satan. He would have been able to perform the same kind of miracles that Jesus performed when people with troubled minds and souls flocked to him for healing. He would have continued Jesus' legacy instead of destroying it.

Manipulation

In 2 Corinthians, Chapter 12, Paul talks about someone he knew 14 years earlier who was caught up in the third heaven where he received revelations. Most preachers will tell you Paul is referring to himself but if you read the passage, it is quite clear that Paul is comparing himself to someone else who experienced a vision. He tells the people he is talking to that he does not want to boast but would like to point out that he has received far more revelations than this person he knew years ago. If one goes strictly by what we know in the scriptures, the person Paul is referring to is Peter and his revelation before meeting with Cornelius. (2 Corinthians 12:2-6)

The reason why Paul feels the need to make this comparison is because the members of the church he is speaking to are doubting his motives. They were asking Paul for proof that Jesus really speaks to him in visions. Instead of addressing their questions directly, Paul threatens them telling them he will not be lenient with them when he sees them in person if they continue to question the veracity of what he is telling them. (2 Corinthians 13:2-3)

When a person holds a false belief thinking it's true, then truth itself can become the villain. Paul's followers were hearing a different gospel taught by the apostles of Christ. Paul disparages these apostles with the nickname *the superapostles* and he describes them as false apostles and deceitful workers, who masquerade as apostles of Christ. (2 Corinthians 11:4-13). Paul begins writing to his followers with the desperation of someone who is watching his influence dwindle and his power slipping away. Like all authoritarians who do not like being questioned, Paul resorts to tactics of manipulation by making them feel ashamed for doubting him. He makes himself into the selfless martyr who has sacrificed so much for their benefit, telling them:

> "Are they [the superapostles] Hebrews? So am I. Are they Israelites? So am I. Are they descendants of Abraham? So am I. Are they ministers of Christ? (I am talking like an insane person.) I am still more, with far greater labors, far more imprisonments, far worse beatings, and numerous brushes with death. Five

times at the hands of the Jews I received forty lashes minus one. Three times I was beaten with rods, once I was stoned, three times I was shipwrecked, I passed a night and a day on the deep; on frequent journeys, in dangers from rivers, dangers from robbers, dangers from my own race, dangers from Gentiles, dangers in the city, dangers in the wilderness, dangers at sea, dangers among false brothers; in toil and hardship, through many sleepless nights, through hunger and thirst, through frequent fastings, through cold and exposure. And apart from these things, there is the daily pressure upon me of my anxiety for all the churches. Who is weak, and I am not weak? Who is led to sin, and I am not indignant? (2 Corinthians 11:5, 22-29)

Poor, poor pitiful Paul. All the troubles he has endured for the cause. This is a tactic of last resort when a very manipulative person feels like his targets are slipping away. They make themselves into the martyr to elicit a sense of pity and shame in the people doubting their sincerity. Paul repeats these admonitions in Colossions 2:1-8 and 1 Thessalonians 2:1-11, where he is once again having to say he has not been deceitful and warning the church not to be captivated with an empty, seductive philosophy according to human tradition and not to the spirit of Christ he is hearing from. What he is telling them is that his word, which he reinforces is not deceitful, is more reliable than the words actually spoken by Jesus. I can only assume the actual apostles of Jesus were the ones conveying 'the words spoken by Jesus.' Therefore, Paul is accusing the disciples who were mentored by Jesus of being deceitful workers.

The 'If You Do Good You Have Nothing to Fear' False Argument

While Moses and Jesus were trying to free their people from the yoke of slavery, Paul was telling those under the yoke of slavery to regard their masters as worthy of full respect. (Ephesians 6:5)

Paul expands on this adherence to authority theme in Romans 3:1-3, where he writes:

> "Let every person be subordinate to the higher authorities, for there is no authority except from God, and those that exist have been established by God. Therefore, whoever resists authority opposes what God has appointed, and those who oppose it will bring judgment upon themselves. For rulers are not a cause of fear to good conduct, but to evil. <u>Do you wish to have no fear of authority? Then do what is good and you will receive approval from it."</u>

Paul's argument that if you do good, you have nothing to fear continues to be a favorite argument of people today who do not seem to care that their individual rights are getting taken away. They say you should not care if your email, phone calls, daily activities and travels are being monitored if you have nothing to hide. Jesus had nothing to hide and look at what happened to him. When the tables get turned upside down, everything gets turned upside down. Under this argument, the burden of proof for wrongdoing switches to the average citizen going about their day. They get perceived as possible criminals until their monitored actions, words and movements prove otherwise. For a targeted individual like Jesus, it can become very problematic when their every movement is known. It becomes very easy for amoral people like Caiaphas to blackmail, harass, stalk or set up an innocent person once they know everything about them and have access to their home, workplace and school.

Caiaphas used Judas to get personal information on Jesus. Spies are a tool of evil. They operate in lies and secrecy. They do not believe in the light of reality and truth. Their lives are dedicated to promoting the darkness of human misery because human problems can only be resolved in the light of transparency, face-to-face communication and truth.

Pretending to be something you are not in order to entrap another human being is conscious evil. It just took a few pieces of silver to get Judas to pretend to be a disciple of Jesus in order to ensnare him. When you make spying a business tied to a paycheck and pension, it does not take long for the network of spies to seep into the entire society with its tentacles touching every soul's life.

In a democracy you are supposed to be innocent until proven guilty. That is why it was a law from the founding of our nation that there must be probable cause for a search. We have created a totalitarian system because people, and that includes citizens just like me, have used Paul's argument to justify the use of warrantless searches every time we travel, write an email or call a friend. We have all become potential targets by accepting Paul's false argument that people in positions of authority are there under God's authority. They are not. More often than not, they are sociopathic pyramid climbers who got their positions using the very same patterns of evil that Paul and his Pharisee buddies used to create their empires and perch themselves at the top of those empires. It is in their best interests to know what the sheep in the rows below are up to so that they can be properly contained. We have willingly enslaved ourselves because of the same fears and anxieties suffered by the Israelites. We have turned our very souls over to people who have no problem in destroying them if it furthers their agendas.

Jesus was calling the Pharisee authorities whitewashed tombs, hypocrites and vipers and Paul was exalting them as appointees of God whose authority should be respected. Paul was at home in the game. Jesus was at home in life. Paul won the game. Let him win. Let all the egoistic pyramid climbers win at their game. It is not worth your soul. Give them the win so that you may live. Do not let them destroy your sense of reality by believing their game is real.

"Therefore, stay awake! For you do not know on which day your Lord will come. Be sure of this: if the master of the house had known the hour of night when the thief was coming, he would have stayed awake and not let his house be broken into. So too, you also must be prepared, for at an hour you do not expect, the Son of Man will come." (Matthew 24:43-44)

Wake up and stay awake. The game we have been told is real has kept us asleep. We are the walking dead on this planet as long as we remain playing the game. The thief has already come and is stripping the house bare. A thief will continue his theft until all the goods are gone or he is forcibly stopped from his theft.

The one thing that can never be stolen from you is reality. That is why Jesus tells us to stay awake. God is reality. God is truth itself. God is us and we are God. Embrace reality and truth. Embrace God and nothing can ever be stolen from you. When you embrace reality you grab hold of the anchor on the sinking ship that has been created by mankind's ego.

Paul's churches were beginning to wake up. It is what caused him to double down on his efforts to silence their concerns. There were bishops, presbyters and ecclesiastics at the Council of Nicaea arguing for the church to include the Gospels containing Jesus' consciousness teachings and they were condemned and excommunicated in order to silence them.[13] The only reason anyone is intentionally silenced using one or more of the patterns of evil is so that the truth does not get out.

The superapostles who Paul ridiculed and the condemned men at the Council of Nicaea were the descendants of Moses, Jesus and Stephen whose faint voices were silenced in favor of continuing the lucrative game. As short as they are in comparison to Paul's letters, I believe the Council included the writings of John, Peter and James in the New Testament because these three men established themselves early on as the builders of the physical church. They, along with Paul, were the rainmakers with regard to building the new religion named Christianity. The church hierarchy gathered at the Council of Nicaea owed their very existence to these four men. It was only right that their legacies should be etched forever in the annals of human history. That is the ultimate payoff for men who love having buildings, roads, schools and hospitals named after them so that their legacies are secured. As for the Gospels of Jesus that were included in the New Testament, there is no way of knowing how much they were edited to conform to Paul's altered doctrine until the vaults are opened and the truth is aired without the threat of having the patterns of evil applied to anyone who airs it.

Writing about Paul has been torturous. It was physically and mentally exhausting. All the bad energy and judgment from the old ladies and men in my church who I disliked so much as a child and teenager enveloped me reading Paul's writings. Yet they were merely relying upon the foundation Paul provided to build his churches. As a child and teenager attending the church, I didn't like Paul's rules or the people who professed to follow them, so I chose to make up my own rules instead. They, along with my own strong ego, helped propel me into the freedom of outer space where I went this way and that depending upon the people I wanted to impress, the job I wanted to get, the boyfriend I wanted to have and the life I wanted to live. The unintended consequences were that I didn't get the results I thought I would because I had no internal compass guiding my way. Happiness was always eluding me the more I tried to serve my own needs and wants – not having any idea what those needs and wants actually were other than what other people told me they should be.

I separated myself from God just as surely as Paul separated God from the members of his churches. And I was miserable. The only time I achieved any sense of true happiness was when my flight through space landed me in a company that had values that matched the ones I never defined for myself and gave me a job and work that fulfilled the yearnings of my soul. When it turned out the people put in charge did not actually share the stated values of the company and I lost my job by following those values, I entered the airspace of ego again. The mental and emotional devastation that loss caused me in the form of self pity, depression, anger, hatred and bitterness almost defeated me.

Our ego's separation from God defeats us all in the end because it splits us from our true selves. Without the knowledge of ourselves that self-examination and knowledge brings, we can never know the truth of our souls and we will always find ourselves looking to other people no better or worse from us to define it for us.

The church has been separated from God for a very long time because it has put God outside of the people it claims to serve by telling them it helps them to find God. Jesus said the kingdom of God is within the individual soul. Only an individual can judge the state of its individual soul in truth.

The church is not the way to God unless it begins to embrace the actual teachings of Jesus which help to lead an individual human spirit to the truth of its real nature. The church Paul created is a lie and to the extent that any church relies on that lie, it is prolonging the human suffering that Jesus came to free us from. There is no branding or marketing in the world that will free the church from the lie. No charismatic leadership will free it. No Pope will free it. Only the truth will free it. Only the light of Jesus' teachings will free it. Only helping each member realize the God within him/herself will free it.

Conclusion

In Mark 10:17-31, a rich man approaches Jesus and asks him what he must do to inherit eternal life. Jesus tells him, "You know the commandments: "Do not murder. Do not commit adultery. Do not steal. Do not bear false witness. Do not defraud. Honor your father and mother." Jesus doesn't tell him to believe in him and he will give him the holy Spirit. He doesn't recite the 600+ laws of Moses that the Pharisees required him to follow. He doesn't even tell him to get baptized. Jesus simply tells him to follow the Ten Commandments. When the young man affirms that he has followed the commandments all his life, Jesus tells him to then give up his riches and follow him. The man cannot do that and he walks away disheartened because he is ensnared by the system that has provided him with so many possessions, but has done nothing to answer the calling of his soul.

It was one thing for the apostles to mask the truth of what Jesus in the flesh told them behind the guise of angels and spirits. It was quite another for a man claiming to be an apostle to change that truth entirely and claim that he received it from the spirit of Jesus. I side with the superapostles who called Paul foolish and false. He was and is. But I also call out the superapostles for being false as well. They should have told the truth of what Jesus did. There were so many Jews and Gentiles who didn't believe people rise from the dead and Paul intimidated the doubters into believing his stories. There is no reason for anyone to continue believing them when we have the ability to determine the truth for ourselves.

People are waking up to truth. The message of Jesus has entered the consciousness of people through alternate means since much of his legacy and personal history was destroyed by Caiaphas and Gamaliel and then later by a church hierarchy which officially adopted the doctrine of Peter and Paul and branded all other gnostic writings as heresy. Whether Paul and Peter were selfish or malicious or ignorant or a combination of all three does not make any difference at this point. It is now up to each of us to determine the truth for ourselves.

We are a global community. All the information anyone needs is out there now. The internet, movies, and television shows I am watching are all dealing with the same age old questions of the Bible. We don't need books or religious leaders to teach it to us anymore. All we need is to focus our consciousness and it will lead us to a path for understanding. There will be no one to blame but ourselves for choosing to remain unaware. These are the end times. We just do not know if the end will bring us to a new beginning or an end to any chance for beginning again. I want to be fully conscious and aware because that is the only weapon I have against an ego consciousness that destroys everything in its path. I want to be awake and stay awake for the hour of our Lord is here. The choices I make going forward will be made with the knowledge that my consciousness creates its past, present and future. I want it to consciously create the vision of God within me because if I can create the vision in myself, I will have fulfilled the law and the prophets that foresaw its creation in the mind of humanity.

The End

APPENDIX I

1. Do not use sharp words towards someone of authority in the church. Rather, talk to them as you would to a father or mother and to the younger men and women, as you would to a brother or sister. (1 Timothy 5:1-2)

2. Honor widows. (1 Timothy 5:3)

3. It is good for men to have nothing to do with women but since the desires of the flesh give them no choice, then every man should have a wife and every woman her husband. (1 Corinthians 7:1-2)

4. It is good for the widowed and unmarried to be like Paul, but if they cannot be like him due to overwhelming desire, then they should get married. (1 Corinthians 7:7-9)

5. A woman cannot divorce her husband. If she does, she is to remain unmarried or get back with her husband. (1 Corinthians 7:11)

6. A man cannot divorce his wife. (1 Corinthians 7:11)

7. If a member of the church is married to a non-Christian and he/she wants to remain with him then he should remain with her. (1 Corinthians 7:12-13)

8. If a member of the church is married to a non-Christian and he/she does not want to remain in the marriage, then let them go and live with one another in peace. (1 Corinthians 7:12-13)

9. A widow without family should pray day and night and if one gives herself over to pleasure is as good as dead. (1 Timothy 5:5)

10. A woman is not to be considered a widow if she is under sixty

and only married once. (1 Timothy 5:9)

11. Younger widows should be married so that they cannot go from house to house talking foolishness and saying things they have no right to say. (1 Timothy 5:11-14)

12. If a woman of faith has a friendship with a widow, she is to give her help so that the responsibility for care does not fall on the church. (1 Timothy 5:16)

13. Rulers who rule well should be doubly blessed, especially if their work is teaching and preaching. (1 Timothy 5:17)

14. Do not believe any allegation made against a person in authority unless there are two or three other people who testify to its truth. (1 Timothy 5:19)

15. Vilify sinners in public so that it puts fear in the hearts of anyone else who may think about sinning. (1 Timothy 5:20)

16. Do not lay hands on any man without thinking about it first. (1 Timothy 5:22)

17. Have no part in another man's sins. (1 Timothy 5:22)

18. Combine a little wine with the water you drink in order to keep your stomach in good health. (1 Timothy 5:23)

19. Slaves should honor their masters in order not to give their masters reason to think ill of God and his teachings. (1 Timothy 6:1)

20. If the master and slave are both of the faith, then the slave should have even more respect for the master and work even harder for him because they are brothers. (1 Timothy 6:2)

21. Men should pray. (1 Timothy 2:8)

22. If any man has been circumcised, let him remain so. And if any man who is a Christian and has not been circumcised, let him remain so. (1 Corinthians 7:18)

23. Women should dress simply with a sense of quiet and seriousness; meaning no fancy hairdos, gold, jewels or expensive clothing. (1 Timothy 2:9)

24. Women should do good works. (1 Timothy 2:10)

25. A woman should place herself in the position of a learner who is under the authority of those more learned. (1 Timothy 2:11)

26. Women should not be teachers. (1 Timothy 2:12)

27. Women should be quiet and never have rule over a man. (1 Timothy 2:12)

28. Women are to be serious in their behavior, saying nothing evil of others and controlling themselves by being true in all things. (1 Timothy 3:11)

29. We instruct you, brothers, in the name of [our] Lord Jesus Christ, to shun any brother who conducts himself in a disorderly way and not according to the tradition they received from us. For you know how one must imitate us. (2 Thessalonians 3:6-7)

30. Avoid foolish arguments, genealogies, rivalries, and quarrels about the law, for they are useless and futile. After a first and second warning, break off contact with a heretic, realizing that such a person is perverted and sinful and stands self-condemned. (Titus 3:9-11)

31. A bishop in the church is to
- have a good reputation,
- be married to only one woman,
- be self controlled,
- be respectful of order,
- be serious,
- be a willing teacher,
- be hospitable to guests,
- not be quick to anger,
- not be a fighter,
- not be a lover of money,
- rule his house well,
- keep his children under control,
- have been a member of the church for awhile,
- have a good name among those outside the church.

(1 Timothy 3:2-7)

32. A deacon in the church is to
- be serious-minded,
- be honest,
- be a moderate drinker,
- not greatly desire monetary wealth,
- be married to only one woman,
- rule his children and houses well,
- keep the secret of the faith in a sin-free heart.

(1 Timothy 3:8-10)

33. Old men are to
- be simple in their tastes,
- be serious,
- be wise,
- be true in faith,

- be loving
- be of a quiet mind. (Titus 2:2)

34. Old women are to
    - respect themselves in their behavior, which means they are not to gossip or drink too much wine and teach others that which is good.
    - teach the younger women to love their husbands and children,
    - be wise in mind,
    - be clean in heart,
    - be kind,
    - be homemakers,
    - submit to the authority of their husbands.

    (Titus 2:3-5)

35. Young men are to
    - be wise and serious-minded,
    - be an example of good works
    - be holy in their teaching,
    - be serious in their behavior,
    - be honest.

    (Titus 2:6-8)

36. Servants are to
    - be under the authority of their masters, doing what is pleasing to them without argument,
    - not take what is not theirs.

37. If you were a servant when you became a Christian, be happy with your situation; but if you have the chance to become free, make use of it. (1 Corinthians 7:21)

38. Servants are to do what their masters tell them, having respect and fear for them as they do of Christ. (Ephesians 6:5)

39. Masters are not to use violent words against their servants, in the knowledge that the master of both is in heaven. (Ephesians 6:9)

40. Be strong in the Lord and in the strength of his power. (Ephesians 6:10)

41. Paul has no orders from Jesus regarding virgins, but his own opinion as one whom Jesus has given his trust to, is that men should remain so. (1 Corinthians 7:26)

42. If married to a wife, do not leave her but if free of your wife, do not take another. (1 Corinthians 7:27)

43. Getting married is not a sin. Although those who do get married will have trouble in the flesh, Paul will not be hard on them. (1 Corinthians 7:28)

44. Those who have wives should act as they would if they did not have them. (1 Corinthians 7:29)

45. For those who are glad, give no signs of joy. (1 Corinthians 7:30)

46. For those who are sorrowful, give no signs of it. (1 Corinthians 7:30)

47. For those who have property, act like you have nothing. (1 Corinthians 7:30)

48. When a husband dies, a woman may remarry as long as long as she marries a Christian. But it is Paul's opinion since it "seems to him that he has the Spirit of God" that it would be better for her to

remain unmarried. (1 Corinthians 7:39-40)

49. Wives are to remain under the rule of their husbands in all things. (Ephesians 5:24)

50. Husbands should have love for their wives. (Ephesians 5:28)

51. There is to be no bad behavior or foolish talk. Replace foolish words with words of praise. (Ephesians 5:4)

52. Children do what your mothers and fathers order. (Ephesians 6:1)

53. Fathers are not to make their children angry. Rather, they are to train them in the teaching and fear of the Lord. (Ephesians 6:4)

And these are my orders for all the churches.
(1 Corinthians 7:18)

BIBLIOGRAPHY

[Unless other wise indicated, all verses quoted from the Bible are from
The New American Bible, St. Joseph Edition]

1 Wake, William (2012-05-17). Forbidden books of the original New
Testament (p. 119-120). Kindle Edition.

2 Wake, William (2012-05-17). Forbidden books of the original New
Testament (pp. 143-145). Kindle Edition.

3 Wake, William (2012-05-17). Forbidden books of the original New
Testament (p. 143-146). Kindle Edition.

4 (2011-09-08). The Nuremberg Trials - The Complete Proceedings
Vol: 1 The Indictment and Opening Statements (The Third Reich from
Original Sources) (Kindle Locations 233-237). Coda Books Ltd. Kindle
Edition

Shirer, William (2011-10-23). The Rise and Fall of the Third Reich (p.
262). RosettaBooks. Kindle Edition.

5 Shirer, William (2011-10-23). The Rise and Fall of the Third Reich
(pp. 268-269). RosettaBooks. Kindle Edition.

6 Meyer, Marvin W. (2009-08-27). The Gnostic Gospels of Jesus (p.
40). HarperCollins. Kindle Edition.

7 Meyer, Marvin W. (2009-08-27). The Gnostic Gospels of Jesus (pp.
40-42). HarperCollins. Kindle Edition.

8 Tabor, James D. Paul and Jesus. Simon and Schuster. 2012.

9 Nyland, Dr A. (2011-06-13). The Gospel of Thomas (p. 18).
Unknown. Kindle Edition.

10 New American Bible, 2 Corinthians 12:7-10

11 Nyland, Dr A. (2011-06-13). The Gospel of Thomas (p. 72).
Unknown. Kindle Edition.

12 Wake, William (2012-05-17). Forbidden books of the original New
Testament (pp. 2-3). Kindle Edition.

13 Wake, William (2012-05-17). Forbidden books of the original New Testament (pp. 2-4). Kindle Edition.

www.ingramcontent.com/pod-product-compliance
Lightning Source LLC
Chambersburg PA
CBHW060803050426
42449CB00008B/1511